CHARLIE CHAPLIN

THE LATER YEARS

By Chris Wade

CHARLIE CHAPLIN: THE LATER YEARS
by Chris Wade

Wisdom Twins Books, 2020
wisdomtwinsbooks.weebly.com

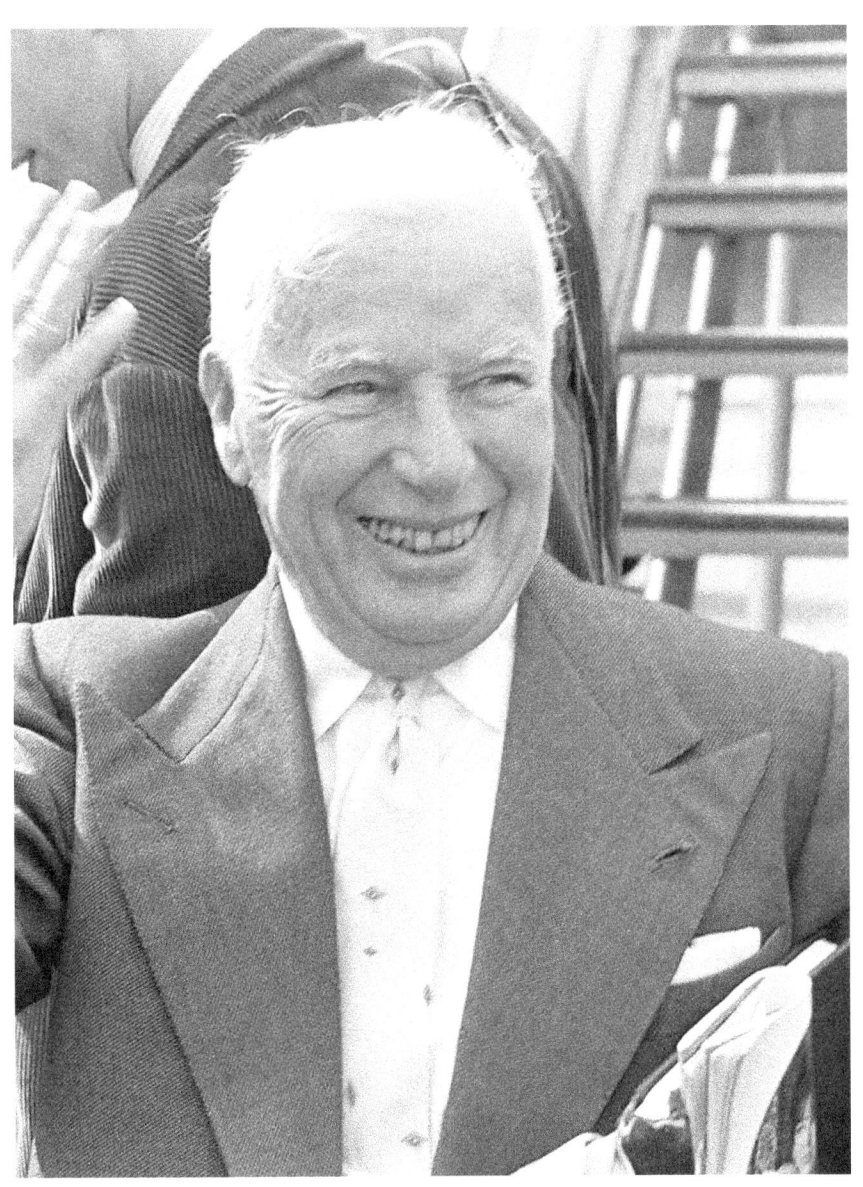

CHARLIE CHAPLIN
THE LATER YEARS

CONTENTS

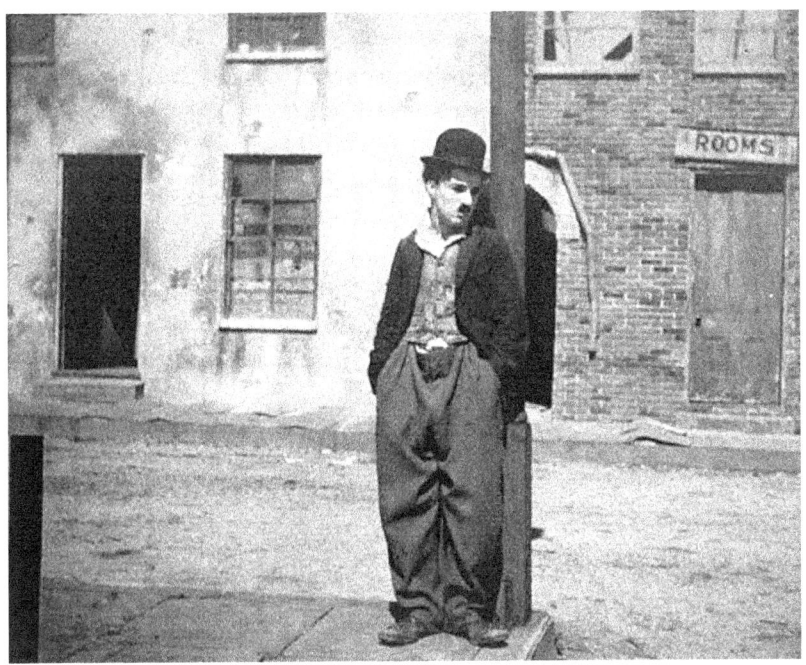

Introduction

"The saddest thing I can imagine is to get used to luxury."

The popular image of the cinematic Charlie Chaplin, with trim moustache, baggy trousers, floppy shoes and funny walk, has been a part of the world's collective consciousness for over a century now. It's an image so strong that it seems impossible that the Chaplin walk could ever be forgotten, and it will most certainly be with us forever. As new fads come and go, stars soar and then fall, celebrities and icons fade into the past, Chaplin's face remains as recognisable now as ever before. He is eternal, as iconic as it is for someone to be and almost beyond legendary, perhaps even mythical now. These days stars of the screen are a dime a dozen, but Chaplin was much more than just a film idol. His pictures spoke to millions all over the world, making them laugh and cry in equal measure. He was also the first real artist of the medium, someone who lifted movies from cheap entertainment to high art. But why have Chaplin's films, the first of which were released in 1914, remained so relevant when those of many of his contemporaries have disappeared into time? Though the Chaplin mystery cannot be defined or fully explained - indeed, nor can his miraculous rise from homeless London child to worldwide mega star and beloved hero - the fact his films connected so consistently with the public, and for the most part with Charlie in the guise of our beloved Tramp, certainly helped.

As Chaplin aged he decided to leave behind his Tramp, last to be seen in his purest form in the great man's 1936 masterpiece, Modern Times. Now sound had come into the movies and the world itself had altered beyond recognition, the Tramp seemed out of place, a voiceless ghost of the past reminding us of a purer and more wholesome time. Chaplin tried out other guises and explored sound, though at first reluctantly and always in his own unique way, moving on as a true artist should. As the decades went on, Chaplin's name in the States was dragged through the mud, due to a paternal suit that wrecked his reputation and his supposed communist leanings, which during the McCarthy era was like being in league with Satan himself. Yet in Europe and elsewhere he remained just as loved and famous as ever before, even as the last sighting of the relatable yet strangely enigmatic Tramp slipped further and further into the past.

Charlie's latter years are a most fascinating time. Thankfully, after years of controversy and personal unrest, the final three decades of Chaplin's life were the most joyous he had ever seen, at least behind closed doors. The press demonized him as a perverse commie from the early forties on, but away from the flash bulbs he met and married Oona O'Neil, started a new family, the kind of simple bliss he had never known. Artistically, though experiencing a hiccup with Monsieur

Verdoux (1947), he went on to make such gems as Limelight (1952) and A King in New York (1957). He was forced out of America and left the land that had been his home for nearly forty years and moved to Switzerland. He was, in short, a king in exile. Through these years Chaplin continued to live a perfect life at the Manoir de Ban in Vevey, with his beloved Oona and children by his side. Yet Chaplin was not merely a retired, contented family man in his final decades; his mind never stopped working, the cogs continued to turn and the ideas came thick and fast. In 1964 he wrote his acclaimed autobiography and directed mega stars Sophia Loren and Marlon Brando in his 1967 film A Countess from Hong Kong. He also travelled the world and continued to write and compose music for his older films. He was busy to the end, even dreaming of making new films against all odds as his body and mind began to fail him.

This book focuses on the final three decades of Chaplin's life, beginning in the mid 1940s when he first met Oona, thus beginning a new era in his story, through the making of films like Limelight and the move to Switzerland (by which point Charlie was already in his sixties) and seeing him to his peaceful death in 1977. Though Chaplin's earliest years in Hollywood in the second decade of the 20th century were artistically fruitful, and indeed the glory years of the 20s and 30s produced films that will never die and a kind of fame the world will never see again, Charlie's personal life in these eras was often rather sad, with personal upsets, setbacks and failed marriages. One cannot deny however the peace he found in his later life. Exploring Chaplin's latter day adventures has been great fun for me, taking me as it has inside his world. Here you will find new eye witness accounts from interviews I have done with those lucky enough to encounter latter day Chaplin, and tales which though may have been told before are still as fascinating as ever. This is the portrait of a contented man, who though both haunted and comforted by his rich and varied past, remained in the present and always looking ahead for the next experience.

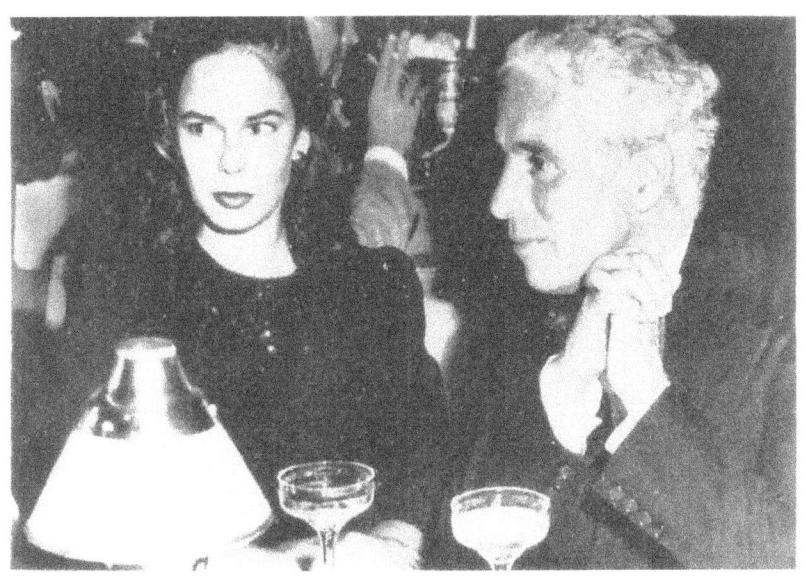

When Charlie Met Oona

To understand the sudden shift in Chaplin's public and personal life in the mid 1940s when he met his beloved Oona, one has to retrace the events leading up to it, including his journey from little known pantomime comic to worldwide icon. Of course, Chaplin had been well known since he first appeared on cinema screens back in 1914 as part of Mack Sennett's Keystone Film Company. His career had gone from strength to strength after his modest beginnings on Sennett's often improvised one reelers. While he had perfected his brand of physical comedy on the vaudevillian stages, firstly in the UK and then in America as part of Fred Karno's travelling performing troupe, Chaplin turned cinema into an art form once he began to direct his own features. When Charlie signed with Essanay Films in 1915 his films became more sophisticated. He established his Tramp persona with a series of increasingly assured productions, but it was when moving on to Mutual in 1916, for a very large sum of money indeed, that his work really took off. Granted, while still with Sennett his films were fairly limited gag reams, but once freed from his contract and allowed to advance technically, aesthetically and emotionally, his pictures became an artful amalgamation of tragedy, drama, comedy and pantomime. These were movies with plenty of laughs but a lot of heart too, and they reached out to the human soul in their delicacy and beauty.

By then, Charlie was known all over the world and whenever he tried to travel he was mobbed by the adoring public. Though he had always wished for some kind of stable success, due largely to his deprived childhood in London, now he found fame suffocating, and as the old tale goes, felt more alone and isolated amidst the crowds reaching out for a piece of him. As the twenties went on, Chaplin reached an arguable peak in his artistry, but several low points in his personal life. As he carved seminal shorts in the form of Shoulder Arms and A Dog's Life, not to mention making the full length The Kid (1921), to some the finest film of his career, he married Mildred Harris in a doomed union that lasted a mere two years. He wed again in 1924 to the young Lita Grey, with whom he had two sons (Charlie Jr. and Sydney), while putting together his masterpiece comedy The Gold Rush, released in 1925. Two years later he and Lita were divorced, Charlie had nearly suffered a mental breakdown and Grey got what was then the largest divorce settlement in American history. The scandal of his divorce, and the very vivid statement released by Lita detailing intimate details of Charlie, even down to his sexual preferences, became a hit on the underground book market. Still, such was his popularity that Chaplin's reputation remained intact.

After making The Circus in 1927, released the following year, Chaplin put his all into his next feature, City Lights (1931), a film which took 21 months to finish (Chaplin said he had worked himself into a neurotic state of desiring perfection). He later entered a relationship with

Paulette Godard, who was the star of his 1935 masterpiece Modern Times. They had married in secret, a detail Charlie only revealed later, and though they remained on good terms together as friends, their marriage fizzled out. Modern Times had been his statement on modern labour, a pre-1984 portrait of a society where workers are observed at all times, kept in line with a brutal regime and even forced to eat while slaving, to ensure no work time is wasted. After this classic (in my view it was a film of brilliant moments rather than a wholly cohesive work), Charlie embarked on a film damning a certain contemporary political figure who was gathering steam through the 1930s - Adolf Hitler. In The Great Dictator, released to great acclaim and box office in 1940, Chaplin played the dual roles of a Jewish barber and a dictator. The honest and decent Jew experiences harsh persecution at the hands of a Nazi-esque organisation, lead by the vicious tyrant Hynkel. It was a brave move for Charlie to make a film on such a current and shaky topic, but despite being warned against the project, he pressed on. Chaplin later stated that he would never have made the film had he known of the concentration camps and true dark horror of the holocaust.

Even for a man like Charlie, whose life had been reinvented time and time again down the years, his life changed immeasurably during and after the war years. In the mid 40s Charlie was at the centre of a media mess involving an aspiring actress named Joan Barry, who claimed to have had a year long affair with Charlie from June of 41 to mid 42, and to even be carrying his unborn child. In 1943 she came forward with these accusations and took Charlie to court. Charlie had initially seen Barry as a possible leading lady and put her on his payroll as an actress on 75 dollars a week. He spoke of her acting abilities to his sons Sydney and Charlie, stating 'She has a quality, an ethereal something that's truly marvellous... a talent as great as any I've seen in my whole life." Later he said it didn't take long before he realised she was unstable. Barry even broke into his home at one point, alarming

Chaplin who was working in his office at the time. She then went public with her claims and was insistent Charlie was the father of the unborn child.

It was hardly perfect timing. J Edgar Hoover, director of the FBI at that time, had had a grudge against Chaplin for some time and made it his main aim to tarnish Charlie's name in the United States. Desperate to nail Chaplin, in part because Hoover objected to his supposed left wing politics, he enforced charges on him that, if found guilty, would see Chaplin face a 23 year jail sentence. Most of the charges, of which there were four, lacked suitable evidence. The Mann Act trial started in March of 1944, causing Chaplin much upset. Thankfully, given the jury's fondness for him and the shakiness of the charges themselves, he was acquitted and walked free. But it felt like a close call. In what had been the biggest Hollywood scandal since the Fatty Arbuckle murder trial back in 1921, Chaplin scraped his way out of Hoover's evil grasp.

Chaplin became even more of a dirty word in America when, two weeks after the suit was filed, he married Oona O'Neill, the daughter of playwright Eugene O'Neill. He'd met her earlier that year and, as with Barry, showed much interest in her acting abilities. When they wed, fairly quickly after their proposed film project together was shelved, she was 18 and Charlie was 54, meaning he was 36 years her senior. Now the media didn't need to make things up to make Charlie look like a beast - the age difference alone was enough for them to pounce upon the once beloved star. Though the pair were hopelessly in love with one another, the press leapt on the story and Charlie's image took an even greater fall in the US. But Chaplin was fearless. He loved Oona, and she loved him back.

Even though his name had been dragged through the mud, Charlie was content with his young girlfriend. Some have noted the irony in the fact that while one young actress in whom he had seen star potential was making his life a living hell, he was being won over by another. But Oona, as everyone who ever knew her attests, was a person of purity who loved and admired Charlie almost from the very beginning. She had no ulterior motive and was simply content to spend time with him. It also helped that his sons, Charlie and Sydney, approved of her, which meant a lot. (Sydney's approval was important, especially when considering it was he who had spotted Joan Barry when she was sneaking around the house and had obviously been troubled by her behaviour.) Sydney and Charlie Jr. later observed that whenever Oona was with their father she was very quiet, listening intently to whatever Charlie said, and then from out of nowhere would come out with some little priceless nugget of wisdom which betrayed her mere 18 years of age. Though their proposed film project (Shadow and Substance was the title) was shelved, their relationship moved forward quickly.

As he eyed up new film ideas in the early parts of 1943, his personal life sailed along sweetly. Oona and her mother would visit Charlie's house often, and though not living with Charlie, his sons came around too and mingled comfortably with the in-laws. They married in mid June, ignoring the Barry case which loomed in the background. After the wedding they honeymooned in Santa Barbara for six weeks, a break which Charlie must have relished. When the stresses of reality did get to him, Oona would read aloud to soothe him, and in the evenings they went for romantic strolls, apparently unrecognised.

But Barry would not go away, and Charlie found himself juggling a perfect personal life with a hellish public one. The paternity suit went to court in February of 44 when the child, born the previous October, was four months old. Various witnesses were called up, including Oona who had never even met Barry. The last witness was Charlie himself, who denied he had sexual contact with her on the dates she claimed, making it impossible for him to be the father. Charlie's lawyer, Jerry Giesler, later said that Chaplin was the best witness he had ever seen

13

and concluded his memories with the fact that Charlie was so small his toes barely scraped the floor when he was sat on the stand.

The new trial, arranged in the light that the tests proved he was not the biological father, was pencilled in for December of 1944. But Charlie wasn't letting it get the better of him. In May he and Oona holidayed together in Palm Springs, and in August their first child, Geraldine, was born. As the case loomed, he was the happiest he had ever been behind closed doors and away from the flashing bulbs of the judgemental media. Charlie was in his fifties when his daughter arrived, and observers say he held his new born child with as much pride and excitement as a young man basking in the glow of his first baby. Meanwhile his two sons had been drafted into the army. The juxtaposition seems extreme today.

Then came the case and the big wake up call. Charlie however was confident that the test results would ensure his escape from Barry's clutches. The big difference in the second trial though was the fact that Charlie changed his representation. In the earlier case he had Giesler, a legal heavyweight. However, once friends advised him, foolishly I might add, that hiring such a top lawyer might make him look guilty from the start, he downgraded to the talented but much less costly Charles Millikan. Once it looked like the case wasn't going the way he had hoped, Chaplin was heard to cry to the judge "I have committed no crime! I'm only human!" The opposition, led by the lawyer Joseph Scott who wasn't ashamed of playing dirty, painted Charlie as a dirty old man, "a lecherous hound" and cruelly a "grey haired old buzzard". The first deliberation saw an acquittal by seven votes to five. During the retrial however, Charlie was not so lucky.

Once the case was picked back up, Chaplin found himself in the losing corner. When Charlie was officially declared the father, he was ordered to pay child support until the baby, a girl named Carol Ann, was 21. The vote showed an 11 to 1 verdict by the jury, again despite the facts proving he was not the biological father. Undoubtedly lead by the media, and in particular the infamous gossip writer Hedda Hopper who tore him to shreds in her column, the jury were having none of it. Alas, Charlie didn't stand a chance. He asked for a retrial but the judge shot down his request outright.

By now Chaplin was seen as a monster to much of the American public and the media were largely responsible. Never before had a reputation experienced such a drastic and very public turnaround. Joan Barry on the other hand did not benefit from her so called victory. Found one day roaming an obscure part of Mexico, she was eventually committed to a mental asylum where she saw out the rest of her days. She died in 2007 at the age of 87.

Tired out, and perhaps too exhausted to go through a retrial even if one had been granted, Charlie retreated and took joy in spending time with his wife and new child. He showed Oona his old films, most of which she hadn't even seen, and delighted in her reactions. She giggled at his prat falls and Charlie, able to view his work objectively as if he had not even been involved in their making, laughed along with her.

But Chaplin being Chaplin, he wasn't content to rest on his past laurels and simply experience the brilliance of his old classics for too long. After all, he was still thinking about future masterpieces yet to be made. Chaplin made one more film in the 1940s, Monsieur Verdoux, his darkest film yet which perhaps reflected his current struggles in the land that had once embraced him as their own.

Misunderstood, undervalued and often sidelined, Chaplin's Monsieur Verdoux sticks out form his illustrious filmography like a sore thumb. Wrongfully, in my view at least, it's often picked out as a slight misfire, Monsieur Verdoux remains refreshing, a film lacking pathos or sentimentality, with Charlie at his least sympathetic. By the time he made the film Chaplin was in his later fifties and he was aware that the little Tramp could not really work in the body of a man nearing sixty. That said, Chaplin is still trim and youthful in Monsieur Verdoux, but his obvious age, which would have obviously robbed the Tramp of his boyish charm, only adds a strange sinister quality to his face in this deranged, perverse characterisation, sinister not being the ideal trait when playing the Tramp of course.

The poster boldly claimed "Chaplin Changes" and changed he most certainly had. In a plot outline devised with the aid of Orson Welles (who later claimed he wrote the whole thing and Chaplin claimed all credit, merely adding that it was based on a suggestion by Welles), Chaplin plays a character based on real life serial killer Henri Desire Landru. Both men agreed that the concept was Welles', that the Citizen Kane genius approached Chaplin with the groundbreaking idea of him portraying a villainous cad, with the intention of Welles directing. Chaplin however did not want to be directed by anyone else and offered to buy the script idea from Welles, who, low on cash as usual, accepted the offer. Chaplin then made various changes to the script, taking out what Welles believed were the key moments. In Chaplin's version of events however no script was even written, though he did like Orson's idea and offered him 5000 dollars to use it. The pair had a bit of a falling out over all this, and Chaplin later wrote that had he known Welles was going to become so bitchy and insist on taking all the credit he would have denied him even an acknowledgement.

Such complications aside, the film, I feel, is unfairly overlooked and often deemed a failure. On the contrary, Chaplin delivers a sharp performance, delivering his dialogue with relish and getting under the skin of a man that could not have been more different to the loveable Tramp. Reaction was, expectedly so perhaps, extremely negative. After all, the Tramp was more than a movie character; he stood for a time of innocence, hope and optimism. By the late forties he was a nostalgic figure, loved, adored, already firmly iconic in Chaplin's own life time.

And here was Chaplin again, the most adored man in film history, playing a sneak, a criminal, and worst of all, a lady killer. Still, Chaplin masters the film as both actor and director, perfectly portraying this low key psychopath with surprising subtlety and orchestrating some of the most striking - and disturbing - sequences in his whole career.

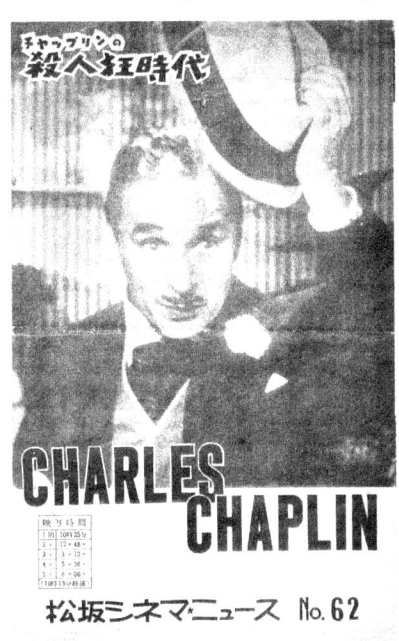

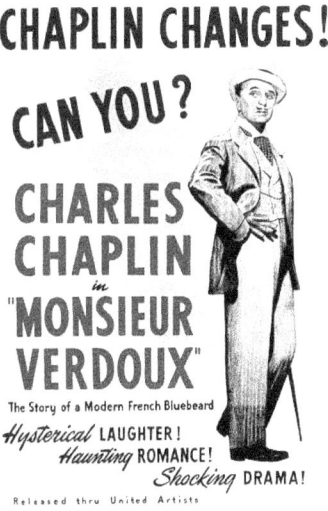

CHAPLIN CHANGES!

CAN YOU?

CHARLES CHAPLIN *in* **"MONSIEUR VERDOUX"**

The Story of a Modern French Bluebeard

Hysterical LAUGHTER! *Haunting* ROMANCE! *Shocking* DRAMA!

Released thru United Artists

Variety, missing the point it seems, wrote in their review that "Chaplin generates little sympathy. His broad-mannered antics, as a many-aliased fop on the make for impressionable matrons; the telltale technique, a hangover from his bankteller's days, of counting the

17

bundles of francs in the traditional nervous manner of rapid finger movement. Chaplin's endeavour to get his 'common man' ideology into the film militates against its comedy values. Point is that depressions in the economy force us into being ruthless villains and murderers, despite the fact we are actually kind and sympathetic. Chaplin also rings in another of his favourite themes, his strong feelings against war. Chaplin's direction is disjointed on occasion, although perhaps the natural enough result of a leisurely production schedule which ranged up to five years."

Most reviews in the US were of this ilk, and the film was boycotted in some American cities, while the reaction was often hostile. By this time however, the increasingly anti communistic, right leaning attitude of the States was becoming ever more suspicious of Chaplin, looking for any excuse to rubbish him and bring forth his apparent shadiness as a character. America, out of love, had previously overlooked the kind of scandals that would ruin the careers of others, but now they not only seemed to be reviling the man himself, but also his work. It seems the hero of The Great Dictator was no more. America needed a villain, and they made Chaplin theirs.

The anti Chaplin attitude began to spread largely due to the Barry case, heightened through Monsiuer Verdoux and then only got worse. Though he is adored today by millions, one could say that that an anti Chaplin mood continues, much less aggressively of course, to this day. An article in The Guardian in 1999 spoke volumes of the turnaround in Chaplin's stature as the greatest figure in film history, when they called him a second to Buster Keaton. Funnily enough though, in the same piece, written by the esteemed Derek Malcolm, he claims Monsieur Verdoux to be the only Chaplin film that matches Keaton's best work:

"There is one Chaplin film, however, which more than equalled any of Keaton's: Monsieur Verdoux, which was made in 1947, and was perversely attacked at the time for being utterly unsentimental. It was

18

certainly provocative. Chaplin played Verdoux, a character inspired by Landru, the real-life seducer and murderer of rich women who operated during the First World War, when eligible men were scarce, and was executed soon afterwards. The real man, though charming, was clearly evil. But Chaplin, moving him forward in time to the 30s, makes him a victim of the Great Depression. Perhaps the philosophy behind Monsieur Verdoux, Chaplin's most pessimistic and gag-free film, was simplistic. But his sarcastic and ironic gravity was astonishing for the time."

As recently as 2008, the New York Times said the film made Chaplin the enemy: "As the cold war coalesced in 1947, Charlie Chaplin's Little Tramp mutated into the monstrous Monsieur Verdoux, a professional bigamist and serial killer supporting his family by marrying and dispatching a succession of wealthy widows."

To sum it up, hopefully not too tidily, those who despise Chaplin's sentimentality and are perhaps a little more cynical may just well relish his turn as the rotter in Monsieur Verdoux, while those in love with Chaplin's softer, more delicate work may find the film a dark nightmare. My own view is not so cut and dry. I admire it of course but would never claim it to be one of my favourite Chaplin works, especially not for the reason that it is not sentimental. The three scenes which for me make it worthy of minor classic status though are the money counting scene, which brings to mind vintage Chaplin, the chilling sequence where he follows the woman into the bedroom at night and resurfaces in daylight (the viewer aware of what has happened through the passing of the night) and when Charlie walks solemnly, looking tiny, towards his certain, bleak death. Though he starred in films after this, Monsieur Verdoux could almost complete the alternative journey of the Chaplin cinematic legacy. The popular view is that the Tramp walked on happily, though inebriated, in 1914's The Kid Auto Races in Venice, and walked away with his love in 1936's Modern Times. Now replace

Modern Times with Monsieur Verdoux, with Chaplin putting the Tramp to death for good, and one gets a totally different view of his cycle. The dream, then, was over.

When the film premièred in April of 1947 Charlie was booed from the streets. It was not a success. During one press conference for the film, Chaplin opened up the floor for journalists with the statement, "Proceed with the butchering." He knew what awaited him.

With the Joan Barry case looming large in the public consciousness, his marriage to the young Oona and now a flop film, matters were made worse when Hoover and the FBI declared he was a full on communist. The Un-American Activities Committee called for Charlie to be deported and in their speech to Congress came out with this sickening statement: "Chaplin's very life in Hollywood is detrimental to the moral fabric of America. [If he is deported] his loathsome pictures can be kept from before the eyes of the American youth. He should be deported and gotten rid of at once."

Despite all the public troubles however, Charlie's personal life was flourishing. By mid 1949 Oona and Charlie had three children; Geraldine born in 1944, Michael in 1946 and Josephine Hannah in March of 49. It was in this period, amidst the conflicted era of being a father again while also being the victim of a savage witch hunt, that Chaplin began writing Limelight, which was to become his next film.

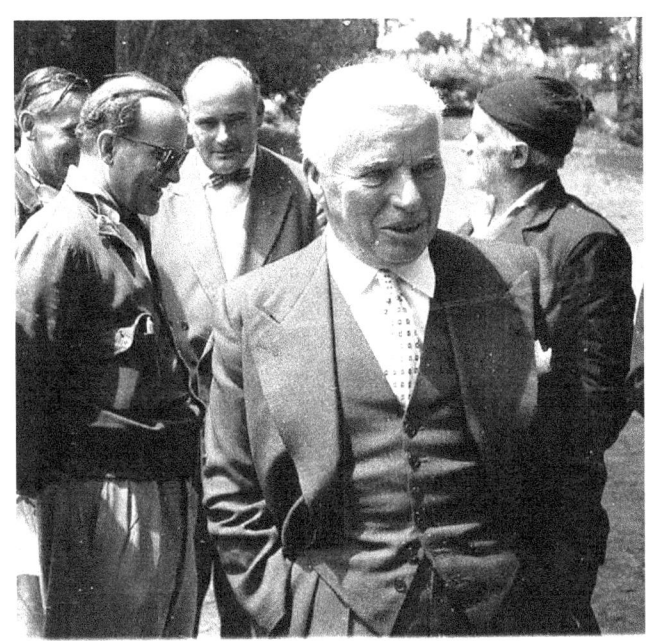

"A Married Man With His Wife and Family": Chaplin in the 1950s

In the early fifties Chaplin and the family were still enjoying life in Hollywood, regularly having friends over for social gatherings, and despite the recent controversies, relishing what appears to be a mostly care free existence. Through 1950 the family would go away on weekends on their yacht and Charlie was now showing his young children the films that had made him a world famous icon. In December of 1950 Oona took Geraldine to see The Gold Rush at her dad's studio, a perfect introduction to Chaplin's films, especially for a young child. The family went on the occasional trip to New York, but for the most part Charlie was working on Limelight, and as usual, throwing himself one hundred percent into the project. According to David Robinson's book, Limelight first shows up in Chaplin's files as far back as 1948, meaning that he spent three years writing it. Originally titled The Limelight, the film was reshaped from September of 48 to September of 50 when he registered the title's copyright. As has now been revealed (and indeed published), Charlie originally wrote Limelight as a novel, called Footlights, a pretty dense one too, focusing on the character of ageing music hall comedian Calvero and the young dancer Terry. His original inspiration for Calvero was the comedian Frank Tinney, someone Chaplin admired when he was younger. When observing him in more recent times however, Chaplin found Tinney was a more tragic figure, and not funny at all. This brought about the image of Calvero, the comic who has seen better days.

Jerry Epstein, a young actor-director who ran The Circle theatre group which Chaplin frequented and even helped out with, recalls having dinner at Chaplin's house one evening and Charlie getting out the Limelight script. He insisted Jerry read it aloud before the gathered friends. When he did so, Charlie promised him that once the film was into production he wanted him there alongside him. "I was flattered, pleased, but didn't know whether he was serious or not." Of course, Charlie was deadly serious.

The original Footlights novel is much more autobiographical than the film. In the book, Calvero wanted to be a musician when he was younger, like Charlie himself, then failed to be taken seriously as a dramatic actor due to his short stature. However, Calvero does admit that he believes himself to be the greatest living actor, a claim many might have thrown Chaplin's way when he was in his heyday. (Indeed, when Chaplin died, Laurence Olivier claimed Chaplin to be the greatest of all actors.)

As Footlights made its way towards the screen, the fundamental story remained intact, though naturally much of the background character detail was left in the pages of the book. Still, fleshing out rich pasts for both Terry and Calvero made them all the more believable when they made it to the screen, giving them a depth they might otherwise not have had. Speaking to his family, Chaplin went into making Limelight with the belief it was going to be his final picture. Perhaps it was the way America was treating him that led him to thinking this way, for he was also considering retirement.

But clearly, Chaplin still loved making films too much to give it all up. Once he had his script finalised he began to put it together. Chaplin took great pride in casting the film, finding fabulous actors to fill out supporting roles, but struggled finding his Terry Embrose. Chaplin was looking for a fresh face, a lithe, shy looking girl who could believably be a ballerina. Showing he was serious about not casting an established star, he placed an advert in the press asking for "a young girl to play leading lady to a comedian generally recognised as the world's greatest." Whether all the girls auditioning knew they were going to meet Charlie Chaplin is anyone's guess, but considering his fame at the time I am sure they were fully aware of who this "world's greatest" might have likely been.

Charlie had been eyeing up hopefuls for years. In 1950, according to the ever reliable Epstein, Chaplin had seen Cloris Leachman in a play and briefly considered her for the role; though as Jerry said, "it was early days". Though Sydney Chaplin was in charge of sorting through the actresses, and Epstein was looking through recorded auditions, the idea of casting Claire Bloom, a then little known English actress, came from playwright Arthur Laurents after seeing her on stage. Bloom was asked to send some pictures to Charlie, but she did not take the request seriously. Much to her surprise she received a letter from Chaplin himself, a rather abrupt one in fact, asking her to send some pictures for his consideration. Upon eventually seeing the photos of this bright young actress, something about her clearly impressed him. Chaplin requested her presence in New York where she was to take part in an audition. Without hesitation, Bloom, along with her mother as chaperone, took a flight to New York to meet the great man.

Bloom said that upon her arriving in New York to meet him, Chaplin instantly began telling her the story and the specific melancholic mood he was after for Limelight. Clearly, he was bringing back the London of his youth, or at least the ghost of it, and he excitedly spoke of the film as he pictured it. Bloom was later struck by the fact that here was this famous man, who could have stayed in Los Angeles and had her go straight to his home, travelling all the way to New York to meet her instead. It's hard to think of any other star, especially one of Charlie's magnitude, doing the same thing.

Through the day, Bloom says Chaplin went over his childhood endlessly, pouring over tiny details and the tragic aspects of the life of the poor in late 19th century London. In the evenings, Charlie and Jerry Epstein took her out for posh dinners, and even while wining and dining at the Pavilion, Chaplin continued to speak of his sad childhood.

Bloom later said that she believed the part of Terry was an amalgamation of his wife Oona and Chaplin's mother, Hannah Chaplin. Indeed, Bloom did resemble the young Oona, but parallels to Hannah are more poignant. The way Calvero heals and revives the young girl is something he would have ideally done for his mother, who succumbed to her mental illness on numerous occasions and never really got over it. Calvero himself is also similar to Charlie's own father. In the book he drifts into alcohol dependency when he learns of his wife's affair, rather like Chaplin Sr., a doomed drunk it must be said, and in the novel he even dies in the same hospital as Charlie's father, St' Thomas on the Thames. There was a lot of his early days in Limelight. It is also fitting that the film itself is set in 1914, the very year Chaplin made his debut at Keystone. While Calvero was struggling through his pantomime act on the dying stage, Chaplin, if the two men existed in the same reality that is, was making a star of himself across the ocean.

Bloom recalled Chaplin going through costume ideas and saying things like, 'My mother used to wear a shawl like that.' If Limelight was a nostalgic look at the music hall era, then Terry was a fantastical version of his mother, freed from her shackles and renewed by Calvero. Even some sixty odd years after she made the film, Bloom still finds it remarkable that this 19 year old "nobody" could catch Chaplin's attention and become his leading lady. Not only was it her first starring role, it was her first film role full stop! Bloom was also struck that, though Chaplin lived in California, he travelled all the way to New York to check out this unknown English girl. Clearly, something in her picture alone triggered an emotion in Chaplin which told him instinctively that she was the right girl for the part. After her audition, during which Charlie enthused about his film-to-be, she had to wait a painful three months - returning to the play she had been acting in - for Chaplin to get back to her. He almost gave the part to Joan Winslow and continued to ponder over his options. Meanwhile he became a father again when his daughter Victoria was born.

To Bloom's surprise and delight he eventually made up his mind and she was cast in Limelight. Once officially a part of the team, Bloom found she was expected to rehearse on a daily basis. Claire recalled there was little room for her own input or improvisation. Almost everything, every gesture and movement, was dictated (playfully but firmly) by Chaplin, who knew exactly what he wanted going in. As Charlie always dieted before making a film, he expected the same from Bloom too. Again, he reiterated the fact that the vibe was to be melancholic, like all of Chaplin's finest work.

Epstein later said that after one particular rehearsal Charlie went into a panic, shouting out "She's to play a ballet dancer! And we haven't even seen her legs!" Once he calmed down, he insisted they subtly ask her to lift her skirt so they could have a quick glance. Claire, apparently wise to their plot, refused. Luckily, Epstein said, her legs were fine.

As far as actual filmmaking went, the trusty old crew were largely gone, and Chaplin found himself with a roomful of new faces. Roland Totheroh, who had been Chaplin's loyal cameraman for decades, was replaced by Karl Strauss. In truth, Charlie hadn't been happy with Rollie's work for a while, though he did keep him on the team, this time as a photographic consultant. During filming it was Totheroh's job to keep Charlie on his toes. At one point he was heard to utter the immortal words to his employer, "Head up... gotta look pretty. Don't wanna see those double chins!" Design-wise it was Eugene Lourie's tricky job to recreate the streets and buildings of Chaplin's London youth, and capturing the look and feel of Charlie's mythical past can't have been a walk in the park. Though the streets do not have the unique, universal quality of those seen in the Mutual, Essanay and First National pictures, they reek of old worldliness, a London that was both totally real and fabled. The interiors are especially fine, Calvero's lodgings being particularly realistic.

Perhaps the most talked about scene in the film is when Bloom's character walks again. When Calvero first meets Terry she has attempted suicide in her room at the lodging house. Calvero knocks the door down and gets a doctor. Terry then recovers in Calvero's room, but is unable to walk. Her big moment back on her feet is a turning point in the film. It is after she stands again that Terry declares her love for Calvero, though the ageing comic knows all too well it is a love out of appreciation for him saving her. Achieving the right feel for the walking scene did not come easy for Chaplin and the sequence was shot multiple times. When it wasn't going according to Charlie's plan, and he felt Claire wasn't nailing it, he criticised her heavily, berating her until she cried. The crew knew Chaplin's aim was to genuinely upset her and then roll the cameras, so being clued up with their boss's cruel but effective technique, they filmed Bloom when her emotions were heightened. In this state Bloom did brilliantly in the scene and finally Chaplin was satisfied.

Epstein said that Charlie liked set ups to be simple and straight forward, blatantly clear for the viewer to ensure there was no confusion. This explains the straight forward shots and camera angles in all his work, especially his early silent movies, admittedly shot in a transitional period for cinema. Here though, despite filmmaking taking on new technical advancements and other directors becoming more visually sophisticated, Charlie kept things basic. Of course, it works in the film's favour; in the theatre scenes one feels like a crowd member, while in the room/bar scenes it feels like we are watching Charlie in a play.

Charlie also famously hated having script girls around and people looking out for continuity issues. Just to wind them up Charlie would apparently change the background mid scene, just to hear them react. "It doesn't match," they'd say. Charlie was both playful and frustrated. "If that's what they're watching," Charlie replied, "then I'd better give up - I have no scene!" (Eagle eyed viewers might notice the pictures on the walls changing throughout the "I'm walking" scene, though by spotting this you'd be going against Charlie's wishes.) Even at this stage Charlie was still conscious of his audience and seemed obsessed by the reactions of his faceless viewers. In one scene, when Calvero talks to a bed ridden Terry, Chaplin appears to have put in a little in-joke about his fans. Asked whether he fears his audience, Calvero replies that maybe he loves them, but soon changes his mind. "I don't love them," he insists. "As individuals, yes, there's greatness in everyone. But as a crowd… they're like a monster without a head. You never know which way it's going to turn." He could have been speaking about the population as a whole, given how they were prone to turning on him.

The same could also be said of the scene in which a dreaming Calvero imagines performing to an empty theatre. Did Charlie feel, after the US controversy, the failure of Verdoux, and the shift in public tastes, that he might too face an empty theatre?

Once the film was shot it took Chaplin three whole months to edit, cut and chop his latest masterpiece, and he poured over the task daily, putting in all the energy he had in him. On 15 May 1952 he prepared and screened a rough cut for the trusted few whose opinions he valued. In early August he even premiered it at Paramount Studios before a very special crowd. A press report claimed "It was the most exciting night I have ever spent in a projection room." All the biggest stars, even Humphrey Bogart, had shown up the take in Chaplin's latest masterpiece. Charlie was greeted like a hero, despite the anti Chaplin vibe going around America.

Those lucky enough to see it in Charlie's presence will have noted the great man had lost none of his ability to move and amuse. Limelight was one of Chaplin's finest achievements, a warm and knowing tragicomic tale set in the fickle and brittle world of live comedy. It fearlessly explored the pitfalls of being washed up, but intent on carrying on because, quite simply, you don't know how to do anything else. In saving Terry from killing herself, Calvero gives new life as his own is fading. The film, very touching and often ludicrously entertaining, proved he had longevity, and that his skill went far beyond the crackly days of silent cinema. Chaplin was still relevant, and the world agreed.

After saving Terry, she becomes a ballet star and is adamant she loves Calvero and wishes to marry him. He knows her love is out of a strange pity and as with his act, the last thing he wants is pity. There is undoubtedly a parallel to how Charlie may have been feeling about Oona. He wanted a pure love, and given Oona was around the same age as Terry it would not be foolish to see some autobiographical subtext.

In the final part of the film we observe the stubborn Calvero busking on the streets before being convinced to make a grand comeback at a benefit concert in his aid. After a genuine triumph, he has a heart attack and is taken to his dressing room. In his last act, he asks to be taken to the side of the stage to watch Terry dance. His friends grab the arm chair in which he resides and take him to observe Terry. In one of the most moving moments in Chaplin's filmography, Calvero dies at the side of the stage, a fitting and poetic finale for a man who lived for the stage and the allure of the applause.

Shot for 900,000 over 55 days, it was ironically set in London but made entirely in Hollywood. Again, it was a case of Chaplin weaving magic, so that it was not exactly the London we all know, but Chaplin's London, completely individualistic. During filming Chaplin was ecstatic with excitement and found it perhaps the most enjoyable on set experience of his career.

Limelight not only brings back the sepia memories of Charlie Chaplin's days in the music hall, it also raises the spirits of the silent comedy era. Though the film is centred in the vaudevillian scene, and focuses on an aged former star, it is the presence of another man which lends Limelight its poignancy and link to cinema's rich past.

Just as Buster Keaton, the faded silent comedy icon, was on the rise as a star of television in the early 1950s, he got a call from an old friend and one time rival, Chaplin. Thirty odd years earlier the two men had been the guiding lights in comedy, with Harold Lloyd close behind, each one coming up with killer film after killer film. Chaplin could unveil masterpieces like The Gold Rush and City Lights, but Keaton had The Navigator, The General and Seven Chances to his name. Chaplin had sweetness, sentimentality and loveability, Keaton had realness, invention, mechanical genius and an honesty that was harsher than Chaplin's Tramp persona. Comparing Keaton and Chaplin is a messy affair though, and one can fall into the all too familiar clichés if you're not careful. Yes, Chaplin used sentimentality to get the audience on his side, but he did so with such beauty that it instantly shoots down the naysayers who use it as a weapon against him. On the other hand, Keaton used his almost unearthly physical skills, his acrobatic abilities, to wow the viewer, but rarely, if ever, did he try to make you like him, never mind feel sorry for him. Keaton left that open; you either cared or not. Of course, some people turn around and say that Buster's comedy is more cold, more one dimensional due to this fact, but I personally disagree. Admittedly, Chaplin was more accessibly appealing, but the mechanics of Keaton's work were as hard to fathom. One could go on all day about the pros and cons of choosing one or the other, if you really wanted to waste time doing so, but the truth is both men were geniuses of their age, and had elements the other didn't, and perhaps wished they had. That said, Chaplin is enduring more than the doubters of the 1980s and the era of the Chaplin downturn ever predicted.

Famously, Orson Welles was always pro-Keaton, and in his conversations with filmmaker Henry Jaglom (documented in the terrific book, My Lunches With Orson) in the 70s and 80s, he waxes lyrical of Buster to a degree that almost does a disservice to Chaplin. Welles had good reason to judge Chaplin though, after a less than satisfactory collaboration (on Monsieur Verdouz of course), but he sincerely felt Keaton was the superior comic, actor and director.

Chaplin on the other hand, was a legend in his own time, a symbol of the universal appeal of good humour, and an icon matched by few, if any, people of the 20th century. While Keaton's star declined in the thirties and forties, and his personal life became messier (he was drinking too heavily, his divorce was ugly and, lest we forget, he was locked up for a short spell and put in a strait jacket), Chaplin's career rose still, so did his reputation as a genius. Buster was popping up in terrible films unworthy of his talent even back in the 1930s and early 40s, and Chaplin was still making some of his best pictures, like Modern

Times and The Great Dictator. Into the fifties, Buster was at least working, but some saw his TV roles as a sad come down, Chaplin included. It was in this period, with Chaplin in his early sixties and Keaton in his mid fifties, that the two men met once again, this time not as friends off screen, but as co stars on the big screen.

The fact that Charlie wanted Keaton in his film is rather telling. Who else but an old rival from the roaring twenties would understand the conflicting sadness and glory of the comedian's existence? Keaton knew all too well the good and bad sides of show business, how you can be on top of the world one day and the bottom of the heap the next. But what made the "reunion" all the more sweet was the fact that Keaton was playing an old comedy partner, whose name we do not learn, and with whom he performs a triumphant routine at a benefit gig.

The idea of pairing Keaton and Chaplin is genius in itself, but what of their scenes together? In short they are magical. The two men, veterans in reality and within the film, look like they know a thing or two and have been round the block a few times, but there is a sweetness to their interaction. Seated before mirrors in the "star" dressing room, Keaton and Chaplin enjoy a marvellous moment applying their make up. Chaplin is confident and happy to be back in the spotlight, while Keaton provides the hilarious cynicism of a faded star. "If anyone else says it's like old times," he grumbles, "I'll jump out the window." The great thing is, of course, that we totally buy it. Unfortunately the scene is just too brief.

Thankfully, the stage performance is longer, and nothing short of a wonder. Keaton, clad in a suit with mad scientist hair and a fake moustache, is at the piano and Chaplin is standing with a violin. Chaplin's loose, Tramp-eque physicality is undimmed by the passing decades, and Keaton's bumbling is fantastic. By the end of the routine, one cannot help but regret they never worked on screen together again, or before this for that matter. But we all know Keaton and Chaplin were too big in their heyday, too iconic and egocentric, too famous and stubborn, to ever share the screen. Here, ageing and more modest, the two legends charm their way into the canon of classic comedy. What is also interesting to note is how each man sticks to their persona, at least in their delivery. Keaton remains stony faced, almost totally emotionless save for a feigned tearful episode after one of Chaplin's moving violin solos, and Chaplin pulls every face imaginable. In one brief moment, they remind the world what had made them the best at their respective, and very different, crafts.

The back-story to the pairing is almost as interesting as their on screen chemistry. Chaplin did not intend for Keaton to play the role at first, for he felt the part too small for such a star. However, when he learned of Buster's personal difficulties he wanted to help an old comrade. The contrast between Chaplin and Keaton's statuses in the early 1950s could not have been harsher.

While rumours have flown about that Charlie was jealous of just how good Keaton was in the stage scene, other people have said the opposite. Chaplin associates have claimed that, in tribute, Chaplin enhanced Keaton's performance and edited down his own, while some say that Keaton really doesn't upstage Chaplin at all, but in fact works with him to ensure the scene is evenly matched. I agree with the latter. In my opinion, there is no upstaging at all, only utter respect between the two silent giants.

Julian Ludwig had a small part in Limelight as a violin playing busker. He later recalled his time on Limelight to Lisa Haven: "If you notice in the scene I'm in in Limelight, Charlie keeps touching me. That's because I was the most inexperienced actor in the scene [the other actors were Snub Pollard and Loyal Underwood] and Charlie directed by action—by touch—and not with words. He kept touching me in order to keep me with him in the scene. That's why I'm the one standing closest to him.

One day, he asked me to go for a walk with him and he took me out to look at his footprints in the cement just outside the door of Stage One. Then he took me into his wardrobe area and showed me all his costumes—the derby hat, the cane, the shoes. Then he took me into the prop room and showed me all the props. After that we walked back onset and into the scene and just started to work through it. There was very little conversation involved. Charlie showed you what he wanted. He knew he needed to make eye contact and touch an amateur actor to keep him in the scene. I thought he was a fantastic director."

He also recalled Charlie interacting on set with his son Sydney. "One day on the set of Limelight out of the blue, Charlie said to Sydney, You know, if I was as tall and good-looking as you, I'd have been the biggest star in Hollywood! Everyone was stunned."

Though Chaplin's methods of filmmaking might not have been everyone's cup of tea, he did it his way and delivered a masterpiece. Now, after showing a select few from the in crowd, he was ready to present his latest masterpiece to the world.

Before the US premiere Charlie spent a week relaxing in New York City, during which Charlie went to see Edith Piaf in concert, even visiting her backstage for a chat after the performance. Among other activities in what proved to be a very busy period, Chaplin lunched with reporters from Time and Life magazine, and also attended a press screening of Limelight. He was apparently uncomfortable during the latter, quite naturally, though expressed some satisfaction that many of the reviews were positive.

The New York Times called the film "a brilliant weaving of comic and tragic strands, eloquent, tearful and beguiling with surpreme virtuosity." Other reviewers, though enjoying the film, found that Chaplin had put too much dialogue in the script. A man who first became famous through his silences was here given a script that would have made an experienced Shakespearean actor sweat. Variety wrote, "As the focal character on the screen Chaplin is, at times, magnificent. He has departed from the baggy-pants but still manages to work in some sock pantomime stuff. However, the role he gave himself calls for too much talk, and some of this grows tedious."

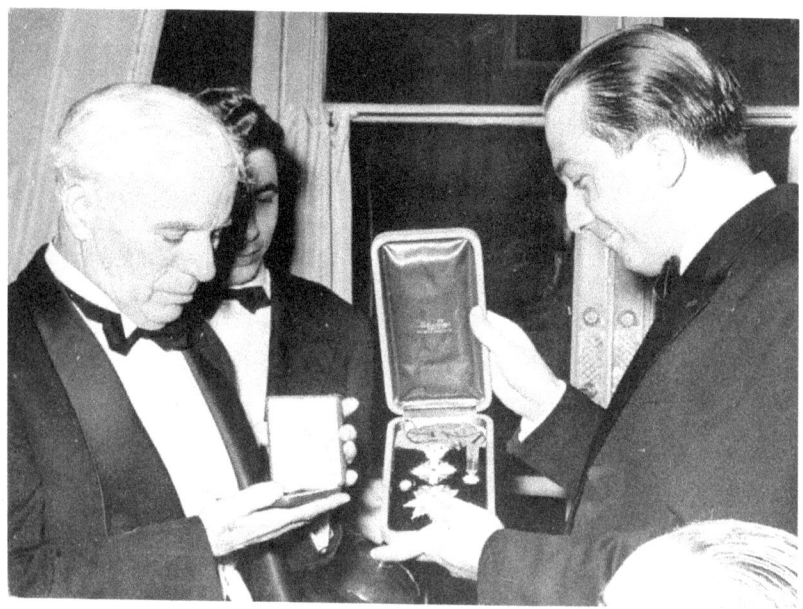

Chaplin being awarded a gold medal in Rome after the premiere of Limelight in 1952.

Even those who liked it claimed it was too long, often too wordy, even if it did deliver the goods on an emotional level. The New Yorker complained, "Regrettably, Mr. Chaplin isn't as quick as Shakespeare in getting the point across. There are, however, rewarding flashes of the sort of comedy and pathos that distinguished Mr. Chaplin's work in the past, and his portrait of an eminent performer who has fallen out of public favour carries a sad conviction."

Today, it's considered one of his best films from the latter days, and it's clear to see why. It had a sadness and a depth that was not only human, but also very moving on a more complex level. Chaplin had made yet another masterpiece, no question, and no one could accuse of it of being schmaltzy. The tragedy here was visceral.

Limelight may be slightly overlong to some, but it's full of wonderful moments, not just the pairing of Chaplin and Keaton, but many of Chaplin's scenes with Claire Bloom too. The film is of great beauty, very poetic and ultimately tragic. It may not be the best place to start for Chaplin newcomers, as it's much less accessible than his earlier features, but it's a worthy effort all the same and up there with his finest talkies. As for his performance, I believe it's a tour de force for Chaplin. Giving himself some truly fabulous dialogue, the comic of Limelight is a clown of wisdom, delivering nuggets of quotable lines with the ease of an experienced talkie actor. He had of course been absolutely brilliant in his previous talkies, as the sinister Verdoux and then as the Jewish Barber and Hynkel in The Great Dictator, but Calvero is so well defined, so well rounded and so real that his words and actions ring long in the mind after every viewing. It's an extremely effective and devastatingly affecting piece of work.

Upon completion, Chaplin came to the UK for Limelight's London premiere. When I spoke to Chaplin's official biographer David Robinson in 2019, he told me all about his first experience, after decades of fandom, of seeing Charlie there in person. "The first time I saw him in the flesh was in 1952 when he came to England for the premiere of Limelight. I was a student, penniless, but somehow I found, I think it was two guineas, for the seat. I had to get money for a hotel and rent a diner jacket, but I went to the premier of Limelight! It was worth every penny, because there he was in the flesh! And he was there with this incredibly beautiful Oona, and that was a huge thrill. So that was the first time I saw him." When David recalled this memory to me, over 55 years since its occurrence, his eyes were filled with joy and excitement at the sheer recollection of Charlie in all his glory.

Chaplin left for England in a great mood, telling a reporter that it felt good to be "a married man with a wife and family on holiday." It was during his promotional tour for Limelight, when arriving in London, that Chaplin learned that America had denied him re-entry into the country. He was labelled a communist, a danger to the American public, and shockingly American theatres, who had once made millions off his movies, banned Limelight and refused to show it. The witch hunt's true aim was clear - to get Chaplin out of America. Chaplin of course knew this was bound to happen. When he left Los Angeles he had a funny feeling he'd not be coming back. He had boarded the RMS Queen Elizabeth on the 18th of September of 1952 and it was the very next day that his re-entry permit was revoked. While on board he told reporters "I have never been political. I have no political convictions. I am an individualist and I believe in liberty." he also passed the time by telling them about a so called movie idea involving a man who arrives in a new country and speaks in an ancient language. He even performed various scenes for them, though he was probably improvising because no records exist of this idea in the Chaplin papers. It was possibly a nice way to pass the time with the press and avoid any more personal questions. He was though, after all, an entertainer first and foremost.

In order to return home (for want of a better word) Chaplin was told he would have to be interviewed about his political beliefs if they were even going to consider letting him back in. Though it was later revealed that there was not enough evidence for such a forceful case against Chaplin to go ahead, and indeed the FBI had no right to refuse his return, Chaplin never lived in America again.

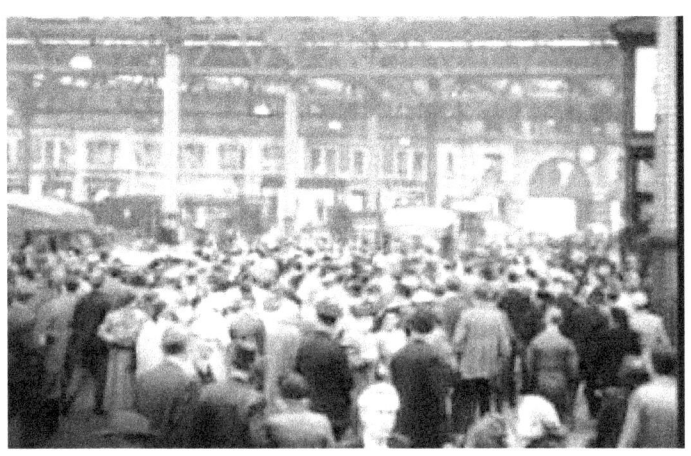

A crowd greets Chaplin upon his arrival in London.

Charlie kept his dignity though. When he heard of the news, his words were as graceful as ever: "Whether I re-entered that unhappy country or not was of little consequence to me. I would like to have told them that the sooner I was rid of that hate-beleaguered atmosphere the better, that I was fed up of America's insults and moral pomposity…" Despite such words, Charlie refused to truly speak ill of America, in part because his home and property remained there, but also because any bad words about the US would only feed this venomous grudge. It's impossible to imagine such a thing happening today, especially to a major star like Chaplin, and even nearly seventy years on the whole situation remains as odious as ever before.

Despite this, Charlie was happy to be in London and eager to show his wife and children the streets on which he had grown up and even slept roughly. He spoke of the poverty but had a strangely nostalgic view of those years too. It was almost as if he were reading from a Dickens novel (his favourite writer), a childhood so sad and deprived it could not have been his own.

But Chaplin's first big act in London was to host a press conference for Limelight. Reporters there described him as "a small friendly man, white haired, his complexion pink" and many seemed surprised for some reason that he did not resemble his famous Tramp character. Needless to say the reporters mobbed him, gathering round for a sound byte from the living legend himself. Though villainised in America, the British press adored and embraced him, while also being charmed by Oona and very much understanding why Chaplin had fallen in love with her.

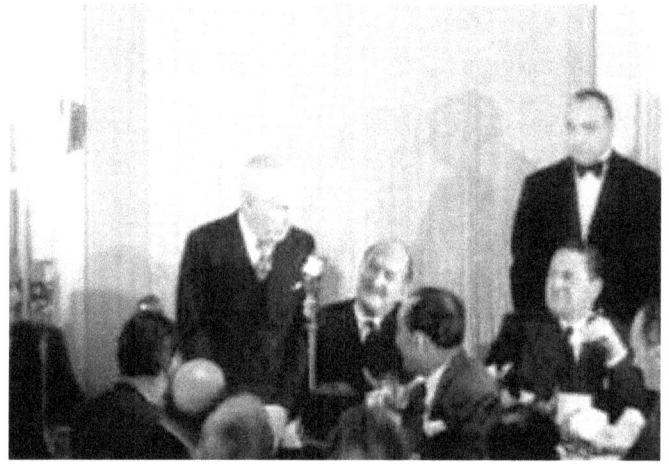

Charlie speaking at the variety Club in London, 1952.

Chaplin and family also faced the press at a charity event. Charlie announced, "We're here for the opening of the benefit for the Royal Society for Teaching the Blind and then after that we have an idea of touring beautiful England and going to all the historical spots. This is the first time that my wife has been abroad and naturally we're going to try and cram in as much as we can."

Later on he spoke to the BBC and expressed his surprise at the recently rebuilt Waterloo Bridge, also stating that Big Ben was "a beautiful sight". It had been 21 years since his last visit and he was clearly overjoyed to be back, especially when he was given a hero's welcome such as this. Claire Bloom later said that Charlie's warm reception was one of the most moving things she had ever seen. But shady business was still at work. Unbeknownst to him, the FBI had messaged the MI5 to keep an eye on Chaplin. Hoover's influence stretched far and wide it seemed.

Chaplin also noted that of his four wives, vitally Oona was the only one he had desired to bring to England and show the London of his youth. The place had a kind of mythical reputation to Charlie and his family, but bringing her to the capital was in a way inviting her inside his heart on a whole new level. No longer a nostalgic, hazy place of mystery, Oona was now seeing London for herself with her own eyes. She also commented to reporters that given Charlie's excitement with being back in London she would not have been surprised if he'd decided to stay. The same day Charlie spoke for the BBC Light Programme he was also invited to the Royal Variety Performance, but being too busy he had to turn it down.

In a speech given at the Variety club he spoke of how London had changed, thanks to the NHS: "I used to look at those little pale faces of the cockney kids where I came from, with their rotten teeth and everything else. One felt impotent about it. Today you have social medicine and I think it's doing a great deal. I've seen rosy cheeked children. Bright, vigorous, active, smiling with confidence. They are the future of England. If for nothing else socialised medicine - if I may say so - is a grand thing for that reason. To take care of our future generations."

From the London premiere, Chaplin and the family journeyed to Paris for the first French screening. While there he had dinner with Picasso and various other noted communists, and later visited Picasso at his studio. While communication was limited by the fact they did not speak each other's language, Charlie and Pablo bonded when they went off together and Chaplin did a comedic routine in the bathroom to a one man audience of the artist alone. He was even treated to a performance of the bread roll act from The Gold Rush. Though delighted at the time, Pablo later spoke negatively of his meeting with Chaplin, saying he had grown old. To him, Charlie was now a man who could not hold a candle to his own idealised image of him as the Tramp. "A lost soul," Picasso dubbed him, adding, "Just another actor in search of his individuality." Picasso was of course being unfair. Chaplin was anything but in search, though his disappointment with the fact that Chaplin had grown older suggests that the ageing Tramp reminded the artist of his own mortality. Indeed, Chaplin's white hair was just a reminder that he took was getting on a bit.

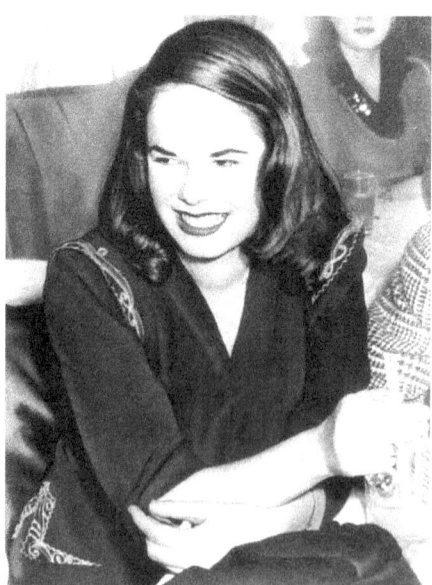

Oona Chaplin.

Even as Charlie was abroad presenting his film to the world he was still ringing back to the studio with artistic decisions and cutting suggestions. Again, the great perfectionist was refusing to let go. Though Charlie himself was not allowed to set foot on American soil, he did send Oona back to oversee their affairs and get their finances out of the U.S. It was while there that she learned the FBI had been investigating the Chaplins and had even questioned members of their staff and anyone to do with them.

Once Oona had sorted out their financial predicament, she returned to the family and they decided, rather swiftly, to move to Switzerland. On the 2nd of December 1952, Chaplin and company flew from London to Switzerland. They were greeted by the press. Footage shot during his arrival shows a happy and smiling Charlie, perhaps putting on a brave face, but a more quietly troubled Oona. He happily answered reporter's questions and smiled as he took gifts from welcoming Swiss children. He told the journalists they were staying for a holiday, at least until Christmas. As the children waved them off, Chaplin and Oona were driven to their hotel.

Chaplin had of course been to Switzerland before, way back in the early thirties, when he'd spent a winter at the Palace Hotel in Saint Moritz with his brother Sydney and Douglas Fairbanks, his closest friend from Hollywood. This was, of course, at the height of his fame. In 2003 Hans Gaartman, who had worked at the hotel in the early thirties, said Chaplin "wasn't as funny" as he'd expected him to be, but was nice and pleasant, even though he was no good on the skis. He also said Chaplin often played pranks on his friends and hotel staff, even once convincing them all he had dropped dead during a party, only for him to get up just as the doctor arrived. Other times, Gaartman recalled, "he would just fade into the background." But clearly there was something he found comforting about Switzerland, and remembering it as a place he eased himself into quite nicely, he returned with bigger plans in mind than a mere break.

Charlie and Oona arrived at their hotel in Lausanne to a small gathering of reporters. One onlooker recalled spotting Charlie by chance as he entered, handed him a notebook and was pleased that the legend gave him his autograph, perhaps the most famous signature in the world. For several months they lived in the hotel while Charlie made up his mind what to do next. Geraldine Chaplin remembered this time as vaguely sad and recalled the image of her mother looking out into the greyness through the window. When the fog cleared though, she admired the beauty of the mountains. Charlie did too and the pair fell in love with the pace of life in Switzerland. Though Michael Chaplin repeatedly asked his mother when they were going back to America, Oona could not bring herself to tell him that they would not be returning.

They were to stay in Switzerland. Obviously the tax relief situation there must have appealed to Charlie, and though he loved London it is doubtful he would have chosen it for his family's home. In January of 1953 they began renting the lavish Manoir de Ban in Vevey. Michael Chaplin later recalled their father taking them to see the house, and he instantly found it impressive. A month later Charlie decided to buy it and it became the Chaplin family's new home for a reported $100,000.

Charlie and Oona oversaw alterations and refurbishments to the mansion, while the cellar was done out to store all of Chaplin's film cans and archives. (David Robinson recently told me of his delight at getting first dibs to go down and pore over the treasures when writing his 1988 biography of Chaplin.) It was at this stage he really began to get his affairs in order. All assets and possessions were arranged to be brought over. He also hired Rachel Ford to be his secretary, an infamously formidable woman who drove a hard bargain and saw to all of Chaplin's legal affairs. Her thoroughness apparently impressed him, even if he was a little weary of her himself. In their initial meeting however she came across as genuinely eccentric. She was wearing one man's boot after losing her own shoe, and had with her a dog on a string, having just lost its lead. She sounds like a Chaplin character through and through. Despite her kookiness, she proved to be a powerhouse for Chaplin's affairs and she stayed with the family for a long time, a loyal face in a world of potential swindlers.

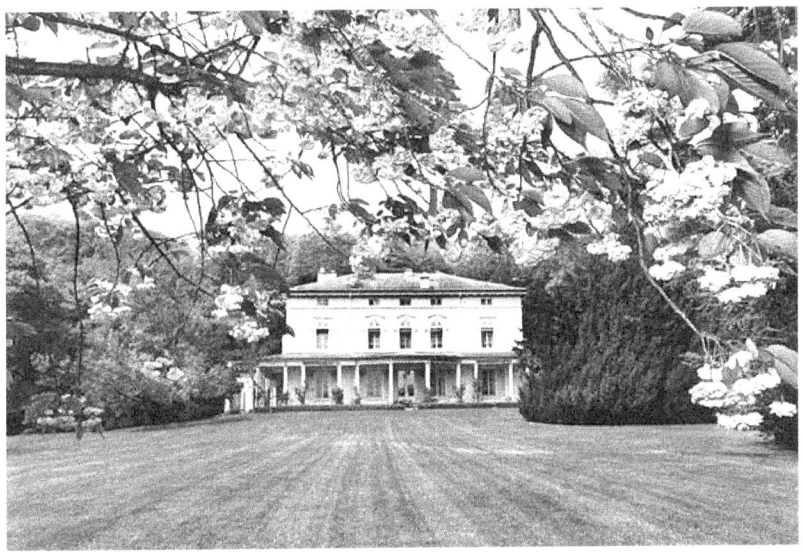

The Manoir de Ban, Chaplin's home in Vevey, Switzerland.

As Ford got herself comfortable and swiftly to work, the Chaplin family settled into the Manoir de Ban. Charlie, wanting privacy, took a break from work and turned down all social invitations, despite being summoned by anyone and everyone of note you could dare to mention. The only thing that niggled Charlie about the house was the noise coming from the nearby firing range. When Charlie had first viewed the house it was the winter and the range was closed, so he was unaware of what kind of noise would come from there in season. In the summer however, it gave off an irritating din, and even the army used it for training. As the years went on, Chaplin made numerous complaints and even tried to have the range closed down. Whenever his attempts proved futile, he would threaten to move and find somewhere else. Of course, he never followed it through and he saw out the rest of his days there. (He later used the horrid sound of guns firing as a gag in A King in New York, when his character is at the cinema and becomes irritated by the cowboys having a very noisy shoot out.) Chaplin meant business about never retuning to America, even if they had have agreed one day to have him back. Showing he was serious, he sold the American house and studio lot for $700,000. "I have given up my residence in the U.S.," he was quoted as saying. The locals in Vevey, of course, loved Chaplin being amongst them, though they were respectful and let him have his privacy.

The following year the family holidayed in London, and Chaplin revisited the streets of his youth. Oona gave up her American citizenship around this time too, and Chaplin himself sold off his remaining shares of United Artists. The USA was behind them now and life in Vevey was a dream-come-true. Chaplin loved his sprawling estate and the children had idyllic childhoods there. Charlie's half brother Sydney came every summer to holiday with the Chaplins, and the children recalled him as a fun, eccentric uncle. Despite being rich, he and his wife Gypsy lived and travelled in a caravan, which was parked in the grounds of the Manoir whenever they stayed.

Though he was planning to stay forever, he struggled to learn French. Geraldine said he was desperate to master the language, getting up everyday with his books and records in a bid to perfect it. But, as she said later, "he found the one thing he could not do. He could never do it." (Indeed, recordings of Chaplin trying to speak French remind one of his Hynkel doing German in The Great Dictator and are vaguely comedic.) In July of 1954 Chaplin sparked more controversy when he accepted a $5,000 Peace Prize from the Communist World Peace Organisation, though the fact he gave all the money away to charitable causes apparently made no difference to the anti-Chaplin brigade. Chaplin was very charitable all his life, but seemed to be even more so as he got older. He also famously visited Lambeth, where he had once been in the workhouse as a boy, and gave the mayor $2000 to hand out to the local poor. Of course, he received a hero's welcome when he arrived in Lambeth, the local lad done good.

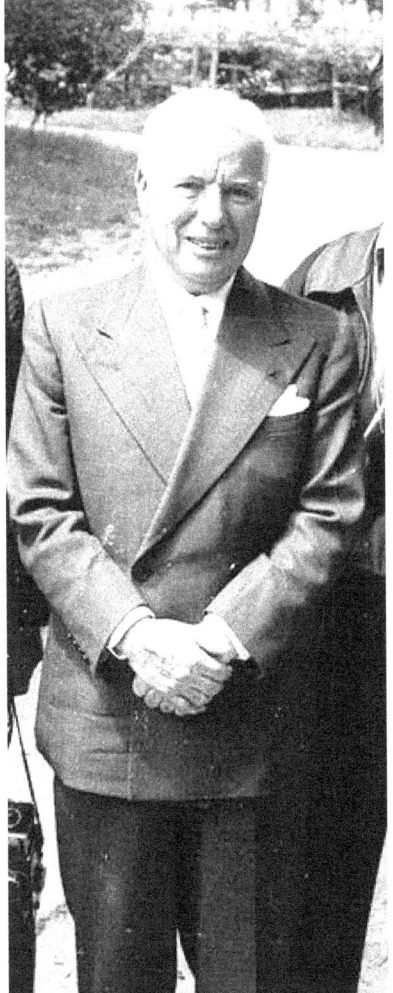

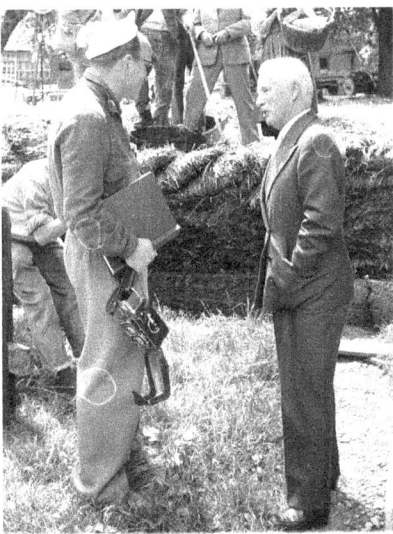

Charlie visits the set of the 1955 film, Ueli der Pachter.

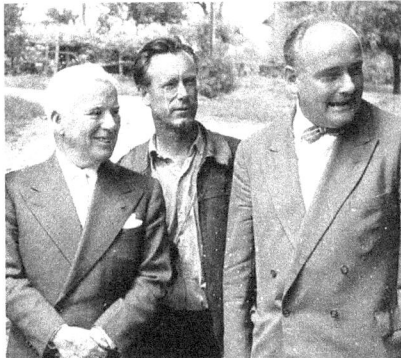

In Switzerland Charlie continued pursuing his ongoing passion for the circus. One piece of newsreel footage from July of 1954 shows Charlie and Oona enjoying a circus event where one of the performers is 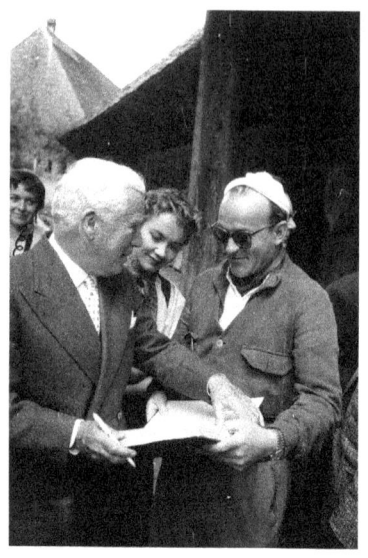 dressed as the Tramp. After the show, Charlie is seen standing to congratulate him on his fine work. Apparently Charlie arrived not as a mere punter but an avid obsessive. His arrival was always early on, as things were being set up, and he expressed a thorough interest in how the whole thing was run. Of course Chaplin had immortalised his adoration in the 1928 classic film The Circus, but it was a spectacle which continued to amaze and entertain him until his final days. The artist Rolf Knie, whose family ran one of Chaplin's favourite travelling circuses, recalled being invited to Charlie's house along with all the other children of the circus performers for drinks and food. They once screened The Circus there too, which no doubt must have been an amazing evening.

Once back in Vevey Charlie began to go over some film ideas he had been kicking around in his head. A King in New York first came up at the end of 53, and all the way through 1954 and 55 he worked on the script, honing it, perfecting it. To help him he invited Jerry Epstein, the man who had been his assistant director on Limelight, over to the Manoir de Ban to move in and assist him in completing the screenplay. Together they set up Attica Films and after more work on the script, the production began.

Putting Chaplin's situation in the mid fifties into perspective tells you everything you need to know about his post US state of mind. By 1957 Chaplin had been out of America for five years, living a perfect life in Switzerland with his wife Oona and growing family of children. Though he had tried to retire, he was unhappy, and Charlie found that coming up with gags, ideas and stories was what pleased him the most, even in his late sixties. Most men of his age and with his wealth would have retired to the rocking chair, only Chapln was far from done at this stage and had plenty left to say.

And so A King in New York was born. The premise was a simple but effective one, concerning the king of Estrovia arriving in New York, penniless, after being de-throned by the government. Now in the bright lights of America (not America in reality, but a London film studio), the exiled king tries to make a living, exploring various ways to earn some cash, including acting in commercials. The plot, loose as it is, seems more like a frame on to which Chaplin can hang his anti capitalist and anti American views. Though never preachy, this is Chaplin's most politically minded film, even though he claimed it was not a political film at all.

Unfairly underrated, A King in New York is not only thought provoking in its prophetic predictions of western society, it is also very funny, featuring some of the most amusing moments from Chaplin's talkie period. The scene in which a newly cosmetically transformed king tries not to laugh at a stage performer, in case it tears his face lift, is hilarious, while Chaplin plays the dignified man robbed of his self respect time and time again with controlled subtlety. Indeed, he comes across as genuine dignitary. Like the drunken Tramp trying to hold on to his pride, the king is at his funniest when being priggish despite his dire situation. That said, the film is perhaps most effective as a metaphorical attack against the anti communist witch hunt period of

American history, a very dramatic and heightened era which ruined many lives and certainly transformed Chaplin's own.

Charlie's accomplished performance aside, Chaplin's real life son Michael has a wonderful part as Rupert, a smart ten year old at a progressive school who has some radical ideas about political change but all too aware of the paranoiac state of his nation. He is so good in fact that it's a surprise he didn't go on to movie stardom after this. "I enjoyed it very much," Michael told a reporter on being in the film. Asked whether he was going to make films in the future, Michael said he wanted to but it was up to daddy. When an interviewer asked Chaplin if he would be happy for his son to be in more films, he shook his head. He stated he wanted MIchael to get an education. Asked whether he would be pleased if he was to take up acting as an adult, Chaplin said that was out of his control. "After all," he said, "we do not own our children. They grow up and they leave the nest." The last statement would come back to haunt him, especially in regards to Michael. As the years went on, Charlie and Oona would have debates over who was the better actor, their son Michael or the great Jackie Coogan who had become an icon in Chaplin's 1921 classic The Kid. Oona, of course, always insisted the better actor was Michael.

The picture was filmed at Shepperton Studios, in all taking 12 weeks and seeing Chaplin up to July of 1956. Recreating New York in a London studio proved to be tricky, and though this is a passable New York, it has nothing on the locations of Chaplin's early films, the Easy Streets and timeless side walks of City Lights in particular.

When one considers the freedom Chaplin had when making his earlier films, the limitations in the making of A King in New York must have been frustrating to say the least. In the old days of course he had owned his own studio, and the fact that he didn't have to rent the shooting space meant he could spend as much time on a scene as he wanted.

Now though, things were different. He rushed his way through the film, and while I personally think it's well made, others have stated that the pressure he was under is clear in the finished product.

A King in New York performed well in Europe but given Chaplin's reputation in the US at the time it did not see a release in America, the country it was so harshly criticising. This ultimately damaged its commercial performance, and quickly, also rather unfairly I feel, it sank into time. In the 1970s Chaplin re-released the film with a new score and it was met with a warmer reception.

Roger Ebert wrote in his 1972 review during the re-issue, "Somehow the word got around that it was a bitter, cynical, anti-American film, made by a man who had turned against the country that nurtured him. All of this turns out to be a lot of baloney. A King in New York doesn't rank with Chaplin's greatest work, but it is good stuff and there are three or four scenes of marvellous comic invention. And it's a hopeful film, more bitter sweet than bitter. Only the hysterical frenzies of the Joe McCarthy era could have made it seem otherwise. Chaplin's political satire no longer seems as daring as it must have been in the 1950s, but his social commentary is, if anything, more timely now. It's a relief, somehow, to learn at last that Chaplin didn't bow out in bitterness, and that the last film he starred in was as gentle, optimistic and funny as the first."

Clearly it was a film which would make much more sense to Americans when all the fuss of the McCarthy era had died down. Charged not with bitterness but a healthy dose of critical cynicism for a country that had thrown him out like yesterday's trash, this bright, well performed, funny and thought provoking film deserves much more attention than it so unfairly receives. That said, Chaplin always maintained that it was not his aim to make a political film but merely a comedy to make people laugh. If anything though, Chaplin appears to not just be having a pop at American paranoia and politics, but also the media world, in particular TV and advertising, something that didn't even exist when Charlie was making his earliest classics. But if it really was intended as a straight forward comedy, in my opinion Chaplin's film achieved its goal.

It was a brave move for Chaplin to make a film critical of America, considering his reputation there at that time. I doubt that he cared how it was received in the U.S., but it did not help that upon its Paris premiere Chaplin banned all American critics. In the USA the campaign against him continued, and when they embarked upon the first stars for the Hollywood Walk of Fame, Chaplin's name was omitted. Not that Charlie cared. He was busy promoting his new film after all.

In the period of 1957 and 1958 he was very accommodating to the press, giving several interviews. Speaking to ITV in 57, he spoke of working at Shepperton: "I enjoyed it (working in the UK) very much. It was a little disconcerting at first and one is always a little insecure when starting a film. The insecurity is the fact that the film isn't finished, it's just beginning. And like with everything else there is a great deal of luck attached to it. I hope I will be lucky with this one. I had a great deal of fun making it and it's more the sort of comedy I wanted to do."

In 1966 when speaking to Richard Meryman, he addressed A King in New York and how he felt about it ten years on. "Well, as I said, the public influenced me a great deal. And I think, well, I wouldn't want to do anything like that now. Although genuinely I had what I thought was a comic notion. Frankly, I got a good opening. I didn't know where the hell the story was going, but the opening was very good. I think perhaps I went overboard a little bit, because I got into politics and so forth. And that was the time of McCarthy. But I see nothing anti-American in it. It was shown in Europe, but the people didn't really understand it. There were certain things that were excellent. It's a very funny idea to do a comedy on honesty. As I say, I am influenced a great deal by the public.

Not that they're completely right, but if something goes wrong, if they show the slightest indifference, that's me. And you've got to play to the public."

In 1959, perhaps with the benefit of hindsight, he claimed he regretted killing off the Little Tramp and not donning his shoes once again. That in mind, if he had carried on playing the Tramp that would have meant no Hynkel, no Monsieur Verdoux, no Calvero and no King of New York. What though, you might ask, would he have been given had Chaplin seen the Tramp into old age?

Funnily enough, 1959 was also the year he worked on The Chaplin Revue, a compilation of three of his best First National shorts - A Dog's Life, Shoulder Arms and The Pilgrim - linked together with archive footage never previously released to the public and adorned with a new Chaplin score. Not merely looking back on his glory years, Chaplin ensured the new score was an effective one, and also interspersed the joyous comedy with actual footage of the First World War. At the near end of another decade, and forty years since the films were made, the Tramp already came across as a beautifully innocent character, and his very appearance brought audiences into nostalgic waves of joy. Thankfully, the Tramp had aged well and adapted himself to the modern world with skill. The films, the charming A Dog's Life and hilarious yet still moving Shoulder Arms in particular, had not lost any of their power. Critics also greeted the Revue with joy. Long time fans were pleased to see the presence of the mythical How to Make Movies footage, a project Chaplin abandoned decades earlier. Today, The Chaplin Revue is quite possibly the single most masterful Chaplin artefact, especially the MK2 edition DVD which features the other First National shorts as bonus features.

The release of The Chaplin Revue coincided with Chaplin reaching a landmark birthday - his 70th. Chaplin quipped "I don't feel a day over 69." It must have helped that his seventh child arrived around the same time, a new baby girl named Annette Emily. Having youngsters around him at all times, calling out "Daddy!", no doubt kept the great man young at heart. That said, Chaplin's spirits and positivity aided his youthful outlook. On his birthday he was asked by a journalist about his views of the future of mankind. Chaplin replied, as quotable as ever, "I hope we shall abolish war and settle all differences at the conference table... I hope we shall abolish all the hydrogen and atom bombs before they abolish us first." He was sounding more like the barber from The Great Dictator than ever before.

Jerry Epstein, whose book Remembering Charlie offers an invaluable glimpse into latter day Charlie's life, often took Chaplin for drives down to London, where he would roam the sights of his youth. Melancholic, but also strangely nostalgic for that time, he would roam the streets until he thought someone had recognised him and then get back in the car. One time Epstein says he went along a road putting money into the pockets of sleeping homeless men before leaving. On another occasion Epstein said he had been invited to a party and asked Chaplin if he wanted to come along. "But they don't know me," Charlie said, failing to realise that, though they did not know him personally, they surely would not have minded Charlie Chaplin turning up. He was, in fact, very shy in such situations and understandably cautious about approaching social gatherings. Charlie also seemed worried that he wouldn't know any of the other guests.

That said, he remained a social person when he wanted to be. While in Vevey Charlie struck up a friendship with the noted Romanian pianist Clara Haskil. She and her family would visit the Chaplin house every Christmas, and as Geraldine recalled, Clara would play the piano and everyone would sit listening while Charlie wept. After she played he would put on one of his old films. She in turn would laugh and weep. "They adored each other," said Geraldine in 2003. Even though he was a legend himself, meeting and getting to know his idols and people he admired brought something of the awed child out in him. On his first ever meeting with Clara, after viewing her at the piano, Chaplin recalled that he had said "in my rather naive way, you are a great artist!" He later said he had met and known only three geniuses in his life; Winston Churchill, Professor Einstein and Clara Haskil.

The Chaplins holidayed often, and one of their most favourite locations was Ireland, in particular Waterville Village where they stayed at the Butler Arms Hotel from 1959 onwards. When they first arrived, the receptionist did not recognise Charlie and as the hotel was full, turned him away. As he was leaving however the manager spotted Chaplin and urged him to come back. He moved him and his own family out of a suite and let the Chaplins in. They continued to go back for years. Charlie loved fishing there, and Michael later recalled treasured memories of fishing in Irish waters with his dad, though the occasions often veered on the comical, sounding like something out of an early Keystone film. The people of Waterville loved having the Chaplins in their town. They were friendly but they also knew Charlie wanted quiet time. He could have gone anywhere in the world but in most places he'd have been mobbed. Here, though always met with a smile, he was left alone. Years after his death, Waterville erected a statue of Chaplin in the centre of town, in honour of their most famous guest, and every year they have a Chaplin related film festival.

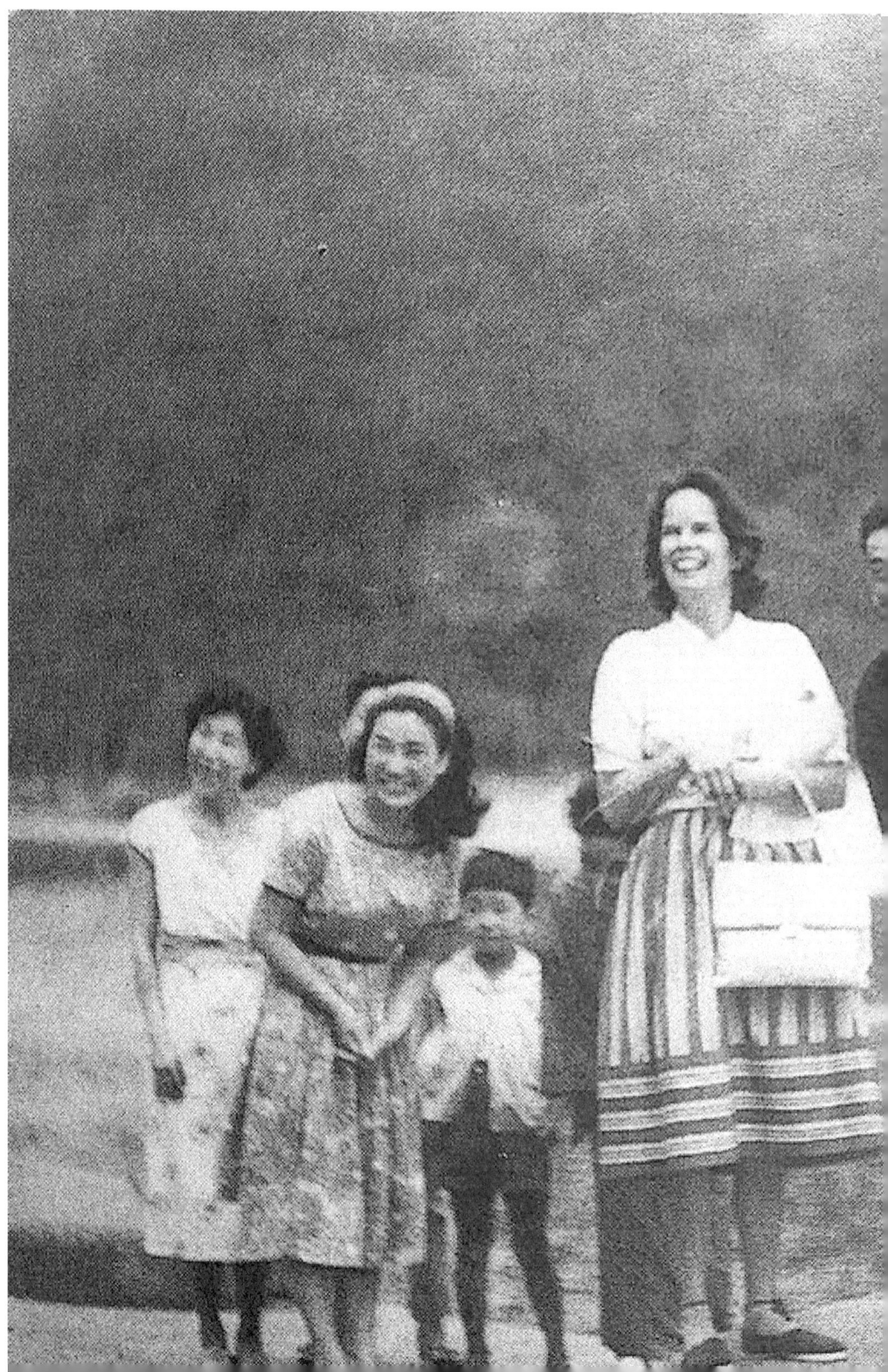

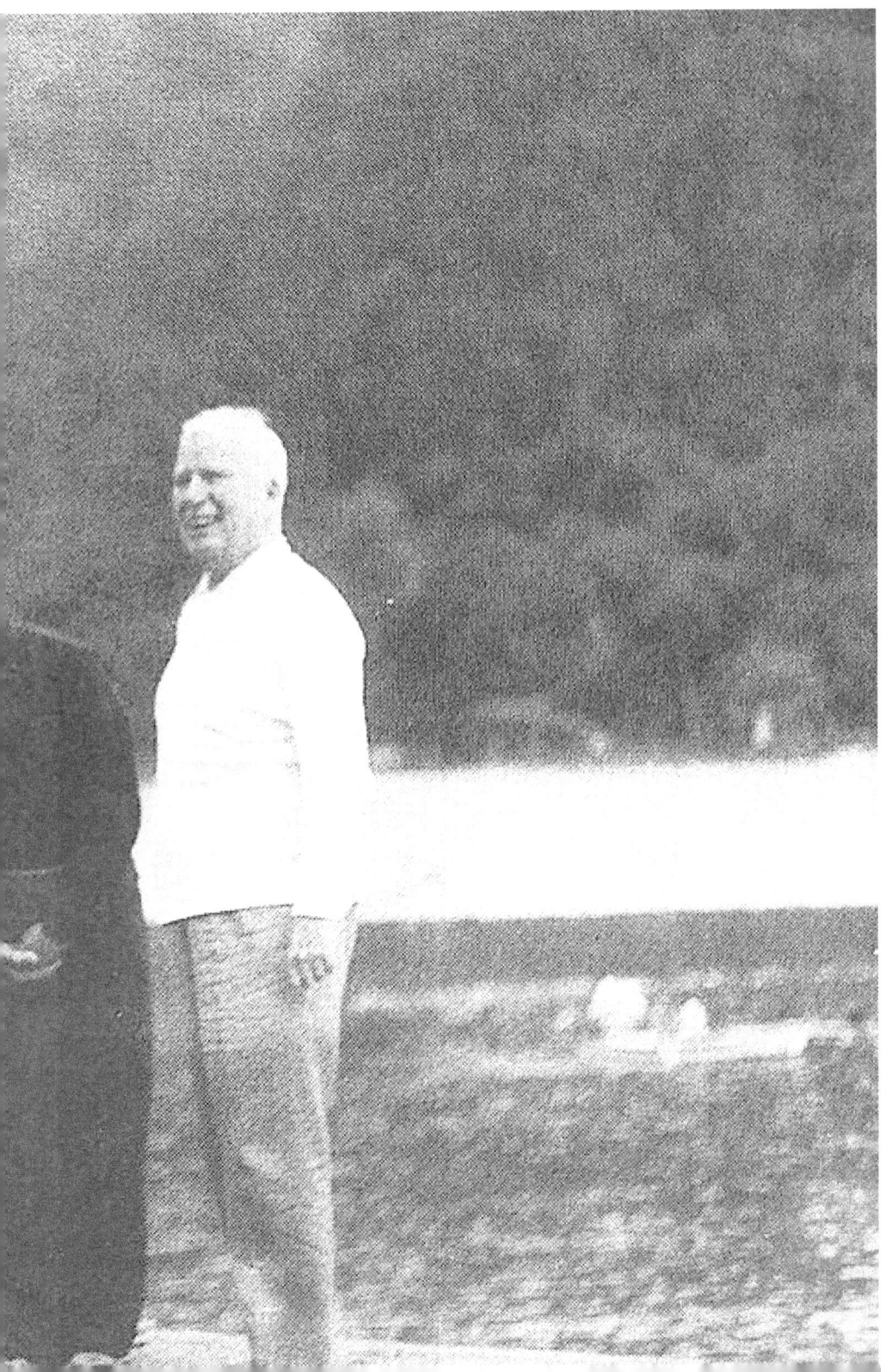

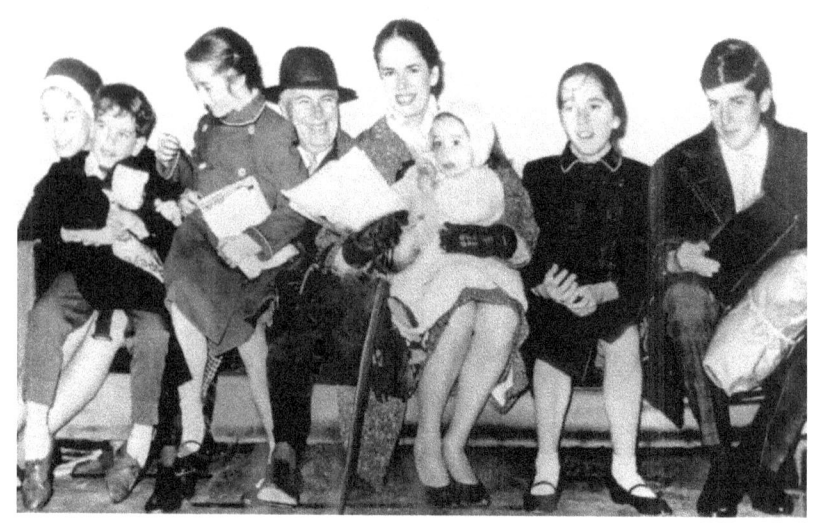

"When it Stops Swinging":
A Man out of Place in the 1960s

By the sixties Chaplin was surrounded by children at the Manoir de Ban and if home movies are anything to go by, he was having the time of his life. As Michael Chaplin later said, Charlie's earlier years had been all about work, work and more work. Now he was getting to play more often, even if films were still very much on his mind. Speaking in an interview, Geraldine Chaplin painted a portrait of what it was like to be a child of Charlie Chaplin: "Children have a very happy life in the Chaplin household. They play and laugh and sing and make a lot of noise all the time, and there's always something going on, an argument, a quarrel. And then mother gives them a lot of her attention, father loves them very much; children are never unhappy, never lonely in the Chaplin house. Everything's simple in the Chaplin household, while you're children."

The Chaplin children have spoken often about their parents and what each provided to the household. "My mother was the backbone for my father. He depended on her a lot," Eugene recalled, while Michael said she spent a lot more time with the kids and seemed more interested in what they were doing than their father. This said, Oona and Charlie were totally dependant on one another, and Geraldine said that the Manoir de Ban was their bubble, a little microcosm of their own. "Daddy was the president and minister of interior, mother was foreign relation," Geraldine said.

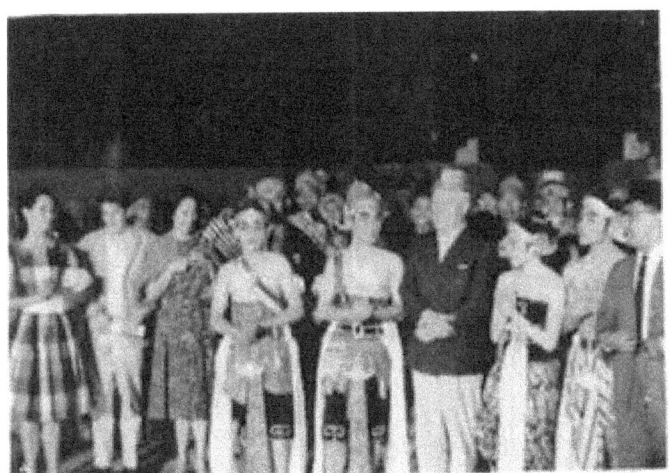

Chaplin attends a function in 1961.

Through 1962 Charlie and the family were all over the place. In the early part of the year they visited the Far East. Later in 1962 the Chaplins went on a lavish holiday, taking in Venice, London and Paris. While in the UK Charlie was given an honorary doctorate by Oxford University. Speedily, Durham University followed suit and he was given a second degree. He was, of course, delighted. He took further joy in the arrival of his eighth child, Christopher James Chaplin, who was born in July of 62. Chaplin was 73 at the time.

Chaplin had many visitors at the Manoir de Ban that year, but perhaps most revealing of all are the trips made there by Francis Wyndham, who wrote about his time with Chaplin. (He also later wrote an introduction to Charlie's 1974 book, My Life in Pictures.) After a 1964 visit he wrote an article entitled "Chaplin At 73, Madly in Love." Wyhdham writes that whenever Oona comes shyly into the room Charlie grabs her hand and shows his adoration. He unashamedly interrupts conversations to declare his love for her. Wyndham also describes Chaplin as a "sensitive, proud, egotistic, touchy man, the essential artist." Frances writes that though Chaplin is an old man he still moves like a dancer. Revealingly, he also describes their private life. "Their front door is sometimes left open all night." Wyndham also says tourists approaching the house or milling about in the garden waiting for an autograph are greeted kindly and politely received. Clearly, he had not lost touch with the man beneath the mythical outer layer. One can only envy Wyndham when he writes that later on in the evening he sat with Charlie on the balcony, who then, as birds hopped on his chair arm, began to talk of his past. In the end though, the article dwells sweetly on Charlie's love for Oona. "It is because of her," writes Wyndham, "that he wants to go on living."

Many have said that Charlie was quite a strict father, though he was firmer with the older children than he was the younger, with whom he fooled and played around. Michael was the one who really rebelled, moving away at quite a young age to London, becoming a tear away, having a brief drug problem (from which he recovered) and writing a memoir based around his relationship with his father. Years later they made up of course, but having such a famous, iconic father was bound to be tough for a young man.

Sydney and Gypsy continued to visit often, arriving in their caravan and bringing a kind of party atmosphere with them. His presence delighted the kids and brought out the performer in Charlie. Home movies show the pair fooling around with the children. Geraldine recalled they would speak in pig Latin and cockney rhyming slang so no one could understand them. Graham Greene was also a regular visitor. The pair had known each other for years, and enjoyed an on-off relationship. Greene's daughter later recalled her memories of sitting down with her father, Charlie, Oona and the rest of the children to watch The Great Dictator in the screening room.

Though he assumed the FBI and their prying eyes were now focusing their attention elsewhere, Charlie later learned that even in Vevey he was being observed closely. The FBI, as had been proven in London, spread their influence across the globe and people were hired to photograph and keep tabs on him, some of whom managed to get very close, taking notes and pictures both when he was at home and attending a public occasion. What threat they saw in an ageing treasure like Charlie is anyone's guess.

Meanwhile, Geraldine Chaplin was just starting to make her name as an actress in her own right, and admitted in one interview that inheriting the great surname was both a gift and a curse to an aspiring performer. "If you want to start a career, and your name is Chaplin, you don't have the slightest difficulty getting started. Everyone reveres you. Nonetheless the disadvantages are equally remarkable, believe me. If your name is Chaplin, people expect a lot of you. They expect too much and you must be good, you have to be, if you're not good they take umbrage, they make fun of you, their respect turns to scorn. But if you are good, they take it for granted and whatever happens you never know whether it's to your own credit or due to your name. Oh! It's hateful to think that, if you do make something, it's just due to your name. It's hateful to think that, if you fail, you'll be crushed with shame:

because of your name. There are times when I think it would be a lot easier to have an unknown name."

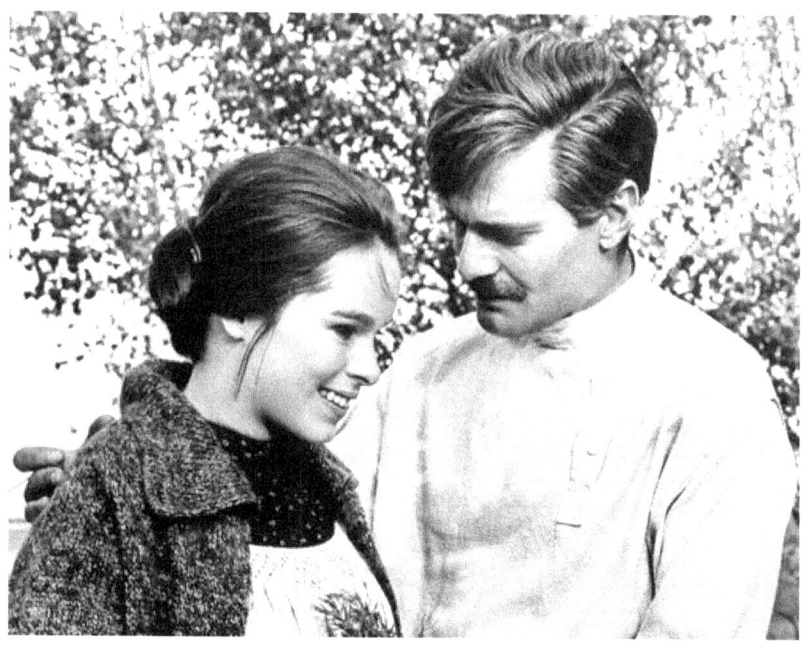

Geraldine Chaplin and Omar Sharif in Doctor Zhivago (1965).

Asked why she had not changed her name, Geraldine was firm in her reply: "Because I'm proud of it, obviously: very proud. Because I'm glad to be Charlie Chaplin's daughter. And also because it would be pointless to change it, it's too late. By now everyone knows who I am. Everyone recognizes me, apart from the fact that I take so much after my father and mother: I have mother's face from my forehead to my nose, and father's from my nose to my chin. Not only that: ever since I was a child I've been photographed with them all, and if I called myself Geraldine Smith, you know what people would say? They'd say: Geraldine Smith, Charlie Chaplin's daughter. The definition of 'Charlie Chaplin's daughter' will follow me all my life, even if I change my name a dozen times. And so, I might just as well go on keeping the name. As Jane Fonda does, for example, Henry Fonda's daughter; or Susan Strasberg, Lee Strasberg's daughter. And I might succeed too: they've both succeeded, haven't they? The only trouble, apart from this positive obligation to succeed, is that you never know whether people give you a contract because they think you'll succeed or because you're Chaplin's daughter."

When the interviewer appeared impressed by all the screen work Geraldine had coming up, the young actress said "It's hard to say no when you are in demand and even harder when your father is Charlie Chaplin and he keeps saying 'do something, do something!' My father paid for my keep when I lived with a family in London, and now he pays or rather he was paying my rent of the flat I've been living in since I moved to Paris, But my father thinks that a girl of twenty should support herself, and I think so too. Obviously I could always telephone home and say I'm in a mess, send me a cheque thank you: but I've never done it and I never intend to. A while back, for example, I was broke: but really broke. But I didn't ask them for a thing."

Geraldine also admitted that she was unsure how her father felt about her being an actress. "I think he's waiting for me at the finishing tape, to judge me... of course if I do fail, I shall face my father and tell him calmly I've failed father." She also hinted that once a child gets old enough they see the complications of having Chaplin as a father. "It's later that things become a bit less simple. It's later that you begin to think for yourself, see for yourself, decide to leave the nest. And so I've left the nest, Michael's left the nest... I was naturally the first to leave it. After me it was Michael's turn and at present he's studying speech and drama in London. After Michael it will be Josie's turn, she's the beauty of the family, fantastically beautiful, even more beautiful than my mother."

While he had looked back to his rich past in 1959 with The Chaplin Revue film, Chaplin agreed to explore his life once more when he began writing his much anticipated memoirs. Records show he began writing them in 1960, taking on the task as he might with a normal work day. He got up at 7 everyday, went for a swim, ate breakfast with Oona before kissing her goodbye to go to his office where he would write until midday. He would then have a nap, write again until 5 and then have the evening off. Clearly he took it all very seriously. Not content to writing a lazy showbiz memoir, he wanted to dive head on into the furthest corners of his memory, especially those in London, bring to life the childhood struggles and contrast them with the often glamorous, star studded life that came in the wake of his massive fame. Chaplin had considered a memoir as far back as 1950, perhaps triggered on by the Limelight novel, but by 1960, at that point with very little view of making another picture just yet, was happy to sit and write. He was, as he said himself, "a content man looking back." He always asked Oona what she thought about his latest passage. If she disliked one or asked him to get rid of it, he would go mad, into a rage in fact, but after calming down would always go with Oona's suggestions.

The book, simply titled My Autobiography, was eventually published in 1964 and was greeted by healthy sales and wonderful reviews. Dickens had been his favourite writer for some time (when he did learn to read, as David Robinson told me, Dickens' books became a major part of his library) and his influence on his own writing is evident. Indeed, throughout My Autobiography, though not concocting scenarios from his own obviously wild imagination, he gives real life events the kind of vivid detail and emotional power much of Dickens' work has. A man of images, famous for his films, had become a man of letters. Oliver Twist was a book that Chaplin read and re-read numerous times through his life, in particular near the end, and in many ways his memoir is his own Oliver Twist. Many have said Chaplin could have made a great screen adaptation of Dickens' rags to riches story of an orphan going through the grime and glamour of London life, one which sort of paralleled his own youth. In many ways, Chaplin lived Oliver Twist and it's all there in his book. Though at the time many questioned Chaplin's story and wondered how much of the childhood section was true, subsequent research has shown his memory was spot on, and save for a few names mis-remembered, it's an accurate portrait of his early life. But it is a part of his life that remains so sad, so tragic, so unrelenting, and so Dickensian that people may not have wanted to believe it was true.

Writing in New York Books upon the release of Chaplin's memoir, F.W. Dupee wrote "his present life as described in My Autobiography resembles the last act of a late-Shakespearean romance. Order has been restored, love is requited, paternity is triumphant, and there has been a general reunion with the universe."

Indeed, there is true poetic beauty in the parts about his current life, Chaplin being a content man who has finally found happiness after years of misadventures. The best parts of the book for me are the early childhood memories and the present day section (Chaplin did once say he was effectively an "entrance and exit man", though he was talking about his screen work at the time), while the glory years are mainly covered in regards to his social life, all the great people he met and so forth, while little detail is left for his screen work and how he managed to create so many masterpieces. Chaplin said he was reluctant to give away details of his filmmaking techniques because it would undoubtedly take away some of the mystery and magic. He was right and though slightly disappointing in this area, the book nonetheless gets you inside Chaplin's head. While Peter Ackroyd in his short biography on Chaplin dismissed My Autobiography rather bluntly

(Ackroyd's book itself felt as if written from a distance, exploring Charlie more as myth than man), David Robinson has praised it as the gem it truly is.

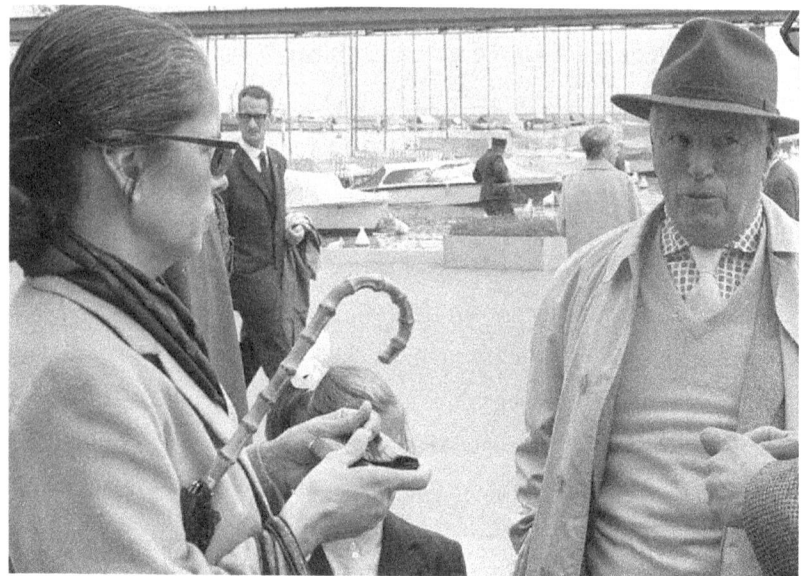

In 1964 Geraldine claimed in an interview that she had not seen her father for a while and was supposed to meet up with him in London for the launch of the book. She said however that her dog Boris was ill and in the choice between her father's book and Boris, the dog won. She stated that she was worried about how her father might view her choice of film work. "I don't even know if father is pleased about this first film of mine. No, father doesn't come here to Spain. father never sets foot in Spain. And then it isn't as if i find it very easy to talk to father, to talk about myself, I mean. Not because he's seventy-five and I'm twenty, I get on well with people of any age, and very young people often irritate me, no, it isn't a matter of generation, it's that father is so strict, difficult... But, yes, perhaps age does have something to do with it."

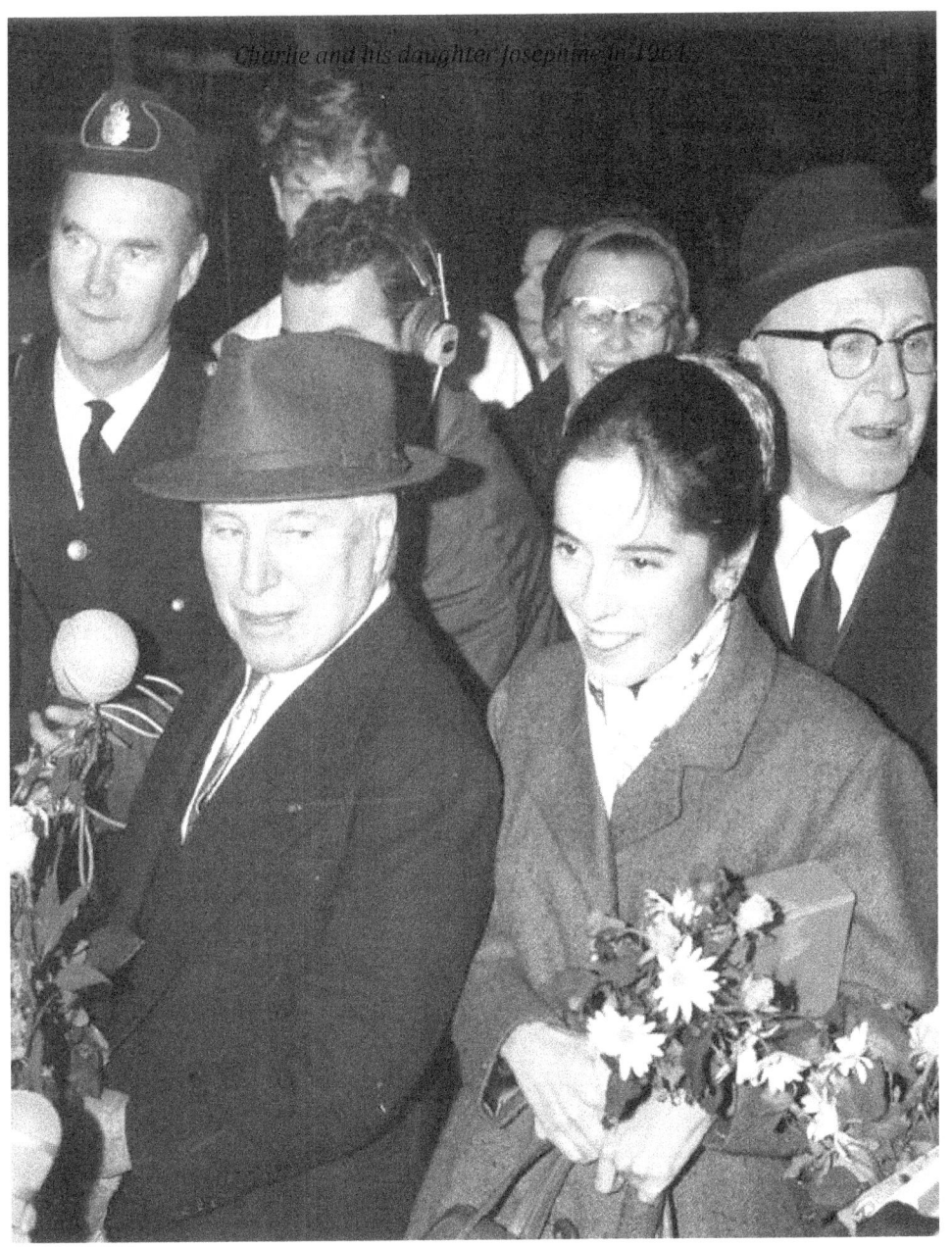

Charlie and his daughter Josephine in 1964.

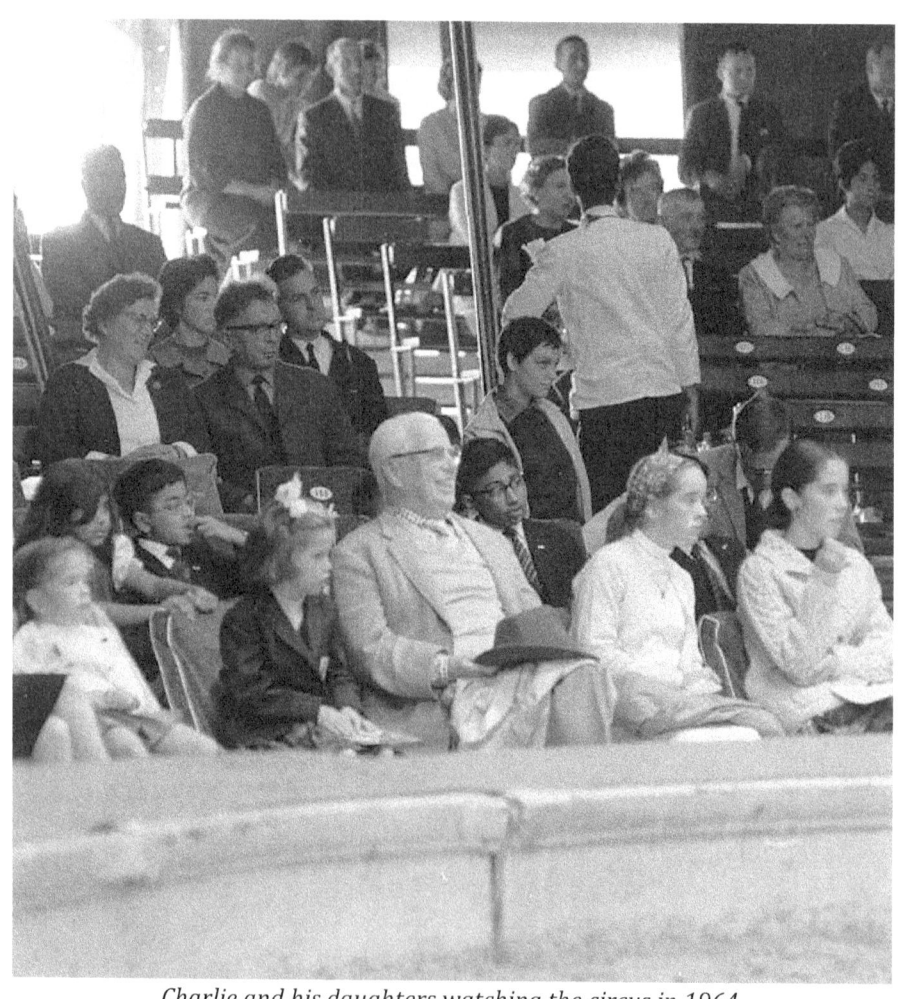

Charlie and his daughters watching the circus in 1964.

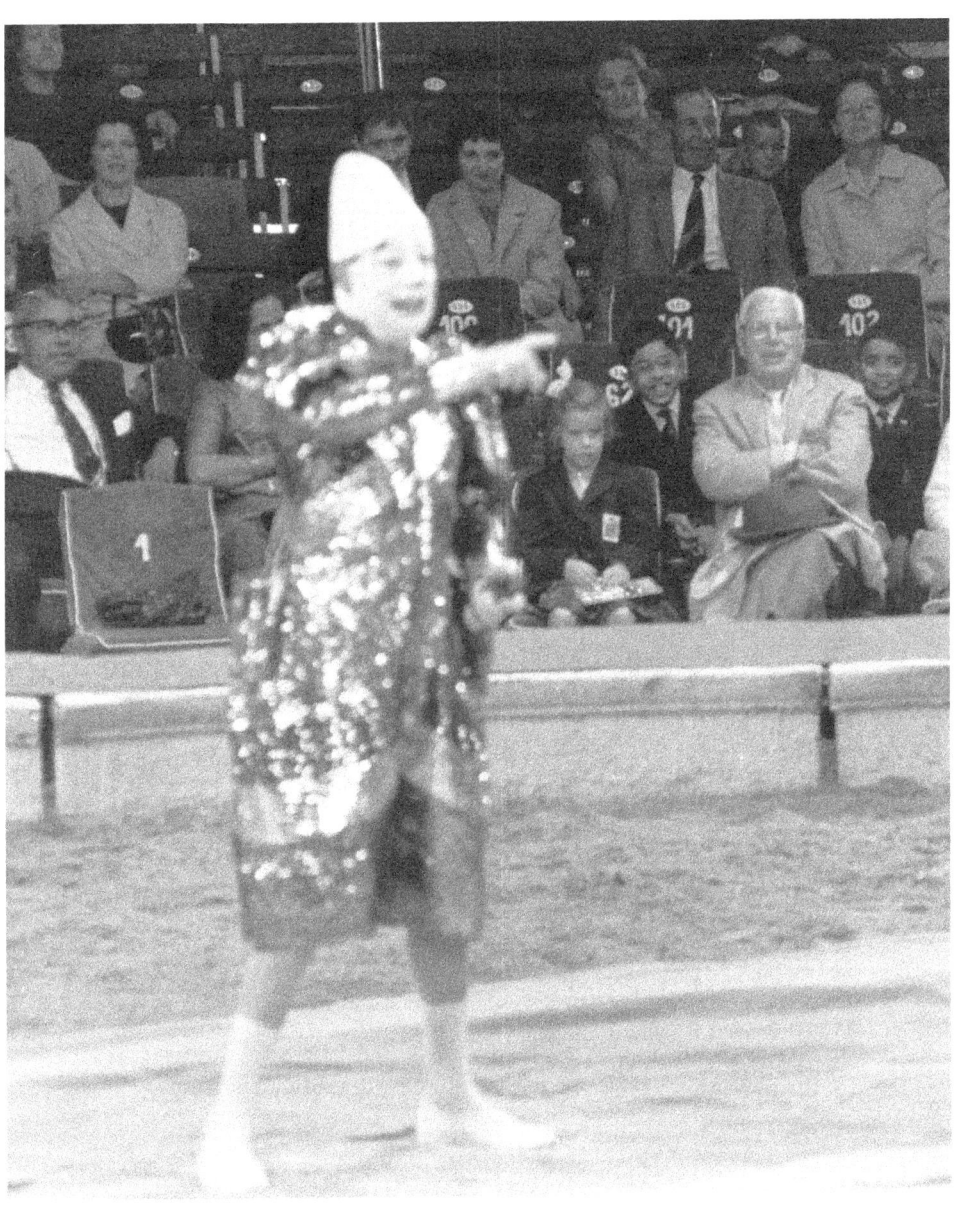

Charlie thoroughly enjoying the circus, 1961.

It was rather poignant that after writing about his youth and in part his relationship with his half brother, that Sydney himself should pass away. The man who had been Charlie's business confidant and very much his big brother, always out for his best interests, was now gone. Ironically, he passed away on Charlie's birthday in 1965, at the age of 80. His wife, Gypsy, was later buried beside her beloved husband. The death shook Chaplin greatly.

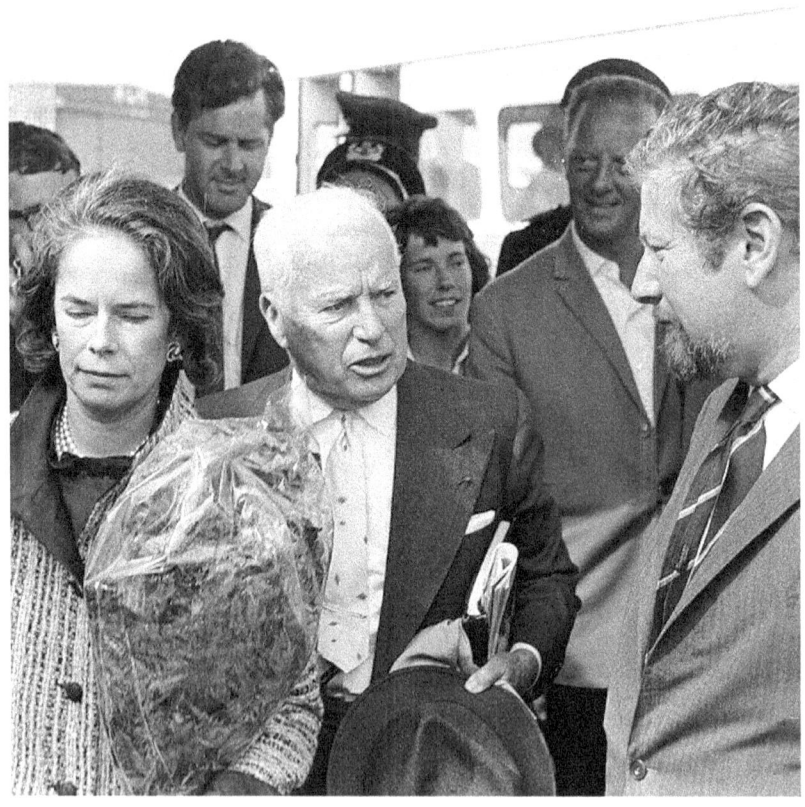

Oona and Charlie with Peter Ustinov in Holland, 1965.

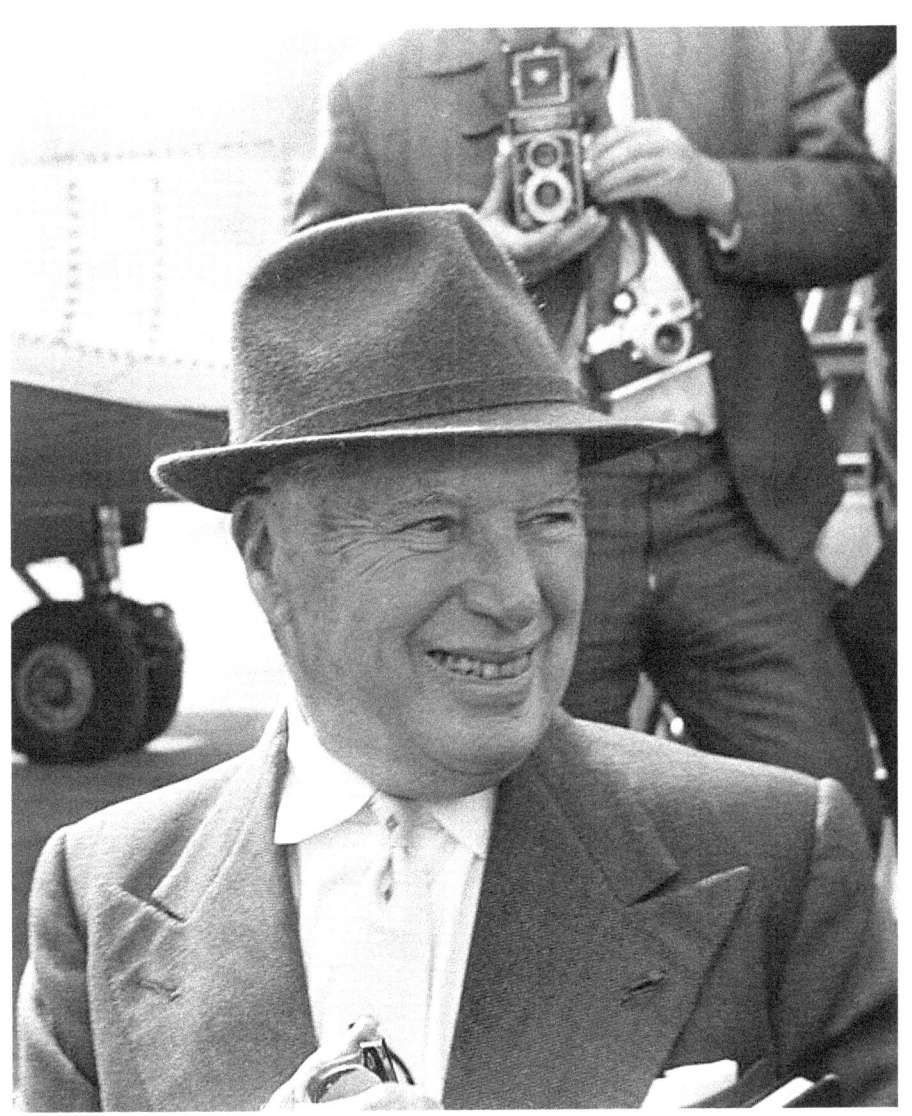

Chaplin greets the press in Holland, 1965.

That year he was honoured in Holland for his work in cinema. He told his friend Peter Ustinov that he had won a prize but unfortunately had to share with a man he had never heard of. "I think his name is something like Burger... Ingman Burger." When Ustinov corrected him and said it was Igmar Bergman, Chaplin said "he's a Norwegian I am told." "No," said Ustinov, "he's Swedish!"

One would think that after all he had achieved in his life, in movies and now in literature, that Chaplin well into his seventies, being showered with honours the world over, should lean back and relax. Chaplin however was no ordinary man. It was after the release of his splendid book that Chaplin began cooking up ideas for his next feature, to be titled A Countess from Hong Kong.

You could fairly apply the word underrated to a number of Chaplin movies, given that personal favourites may not receive the same amount of acclaim as some of the widely lauded masterpieces do, and opinions vary from movie to movie and person to person. But A Countess from Hong Kong is regarded by many to be one of Chaplin's weakest works, to some a slight misfire, and to others, and quite a lot it seems, an embarrassment all together.

Yet upon every viewing I have found the film entertaining, warm, and though far from perfect, both charming and funny, featuring a fine farcical scenario which moves speedily so and a host of performances which are competent considering the constraints put upon the actors in question. Yes the set up is old fashioned, but it's brought into the contemporary sixties by two of the era's finest actors, Marlon Brando and Sophia Loren, who are broad but convincing for the most part. Chaplin directs with a refreshing simplicity and though the set ups often bring to mind the static staginess of television sitcom, while steering clear of cinematic fussiness, Charlie applies his masterly touch so well that 80 percent of it works.

Chaplin originally came up with the idea for the film in the 1930s under the title Stowaway, and it was based on a meeting with a Russian woman he met during a holiday in France in the early twenties. Chaplin also recalled he got inspiration from a 1931 trip to Shanghai where he met some Russian aristocrats who had escaped the revolution, "destitute and without a country." Chaplin said "the men ran rickshaws and the women worked in ten-cent dance halls. When the Second World War broke out many of the old aristocrats had died and the younger generation migrated to Hong Kong where their plight was even worse, for Hong Kong was overcrowded with refugees."

During his 1964 holiday in Jamaica, where Charlie lapped up the sun and swam daily, he told Jerry Epstein about the script and handed it to him for his opinion. Epstein recalled sitting on the beach going through it with Chaplin hovering around his shoulder awaiting his thoughts. Whenever he laughed, Charlie would come back over and ask what had made him giggle. Even at this stage, with tens of masterpieces behind him, he was still neurotic about his work and hoped people would enjoy it. He never became complacent and smug in himself, and that was one of his great strengths as a filmmaker. For a short time he thought about scrapping the film all together but found the idea of starting a new screenplay daunting.

For his two leads, Chaplin chose two of the most loved and iconic stars of their day, Though he was not his first choice, he cast Marlon Brando as the male lead and after seeing her in the Oscar winning Yesterday, Today and Tomorrow, Italian beauty Sophia Loren as the female lead. When Jerry Epstein, once again on board to help Charlie, said that finding a deal would be easy as Loren was so bankable, Chaplin revealed he had never heard the phrase before. He laughed at the word and asked Jerry "Do you think I am bankable?"… Epstein said of course.

In the film which eventually surfaced, Brando plays Ogden Mears, the Ambassador for Saudi Arabia, who is on his way back to the United

States on a boat when he meets the Russian countess Natascha, played by Loren, who has snuck on board after having enough of being degraded in a hall which promises sailors they can "dance with a real countess for a dollar". As Natascha is officially a refugee without a passport, she has to hide away in Ogden's lodgings for the rest of the journey. The situation becomes more farcical as the film reaches its end, and Ogden falls for the misplaced woman, who remains both earthy and dignified.

Mears was originally going to be a presidential candidate in the script, one based on John F Kennedy. However when Kennedy was assassinated he decided to change the script around and make him an ambassador. It was later revealed that Kennedy had plans to lift Chaplin's US ban, so perhaps it was a good move on Charlie's part to steer clear of a JFK-esque character.

Before filming began Chaplin held a press conference in London at the Savoy with Sophia by his side. Charmingly, Charlie had a placard erected there reading "C. Chaplin will be holding a press conference this morning to mark his new film." The place was, of course, jammed, Loren at the height of her fame and Chaplin's appeal undimmed by the passing decades. Apparently, during the event a small number of journalists gathered round Loren as she observed Chaplin surrounded, mobbed in fact, by reporters in every direction. "Now," she remarked, "I know what a real star is."

Though the mood was light, the tide turned for the worse when Charlie got annoyed with Epstein when his young friend kept Chaplin's young daughter Vicky up until midnight. Locking himself in his suite Charlie refused to answer the door or any calls. For a while it looked like the film wasn't going ahead - and all this three weeks before filming was to commence. When Charlie and Jerry made up however the picture was back on. Oona and Charlie rented a country house in the week before the shoot and he invited Sophia, Marlon, Jerry and others to stay while they discussed the picture. Charlie told Marlon he had to lose a bit of weight and the method actor promised he would.

Epstein recalled that Charlie saw the film not merely as a romance or a comedy, but also a statement about power and control. He insisted that people who have inherited money have a more relaxed attitude about their wealth and that Ogden must constantly give off the feeling of comfort, a man who is rich and knows he will remain so. Even at the house though, as Charlie discussed the film with his cast, Marlon appeared to be irked by the director. Epstein said Brando began asking silly questions and that a tension was developing. It was clear that the two icons were not going to see eye to eye. Loren even noticed it too, commenting to Epstein that Brando was clearly trying to embarrass Chaplin in front of everyone.

Unsurprisingly given her performance, Loren had a great time making the film. After all, Charlie Chaplin was one of her heroes, and she seems to have relished every second with the great man. In 2016 Loren said "I was so sensitive and scared to death. My God, Charlie Chaplin. What's happening to me? But I had to overcome so many emotions then went on stage and he was sitting by his wife. He was a very shy person and he was wonderful to work with and a great character. He helped every actor in every way he could. I still remember one day shooting a scene in a big restaurant and I was sitting down and there was a problem in the story, with Marlon Brando's character, and a very emotional scene with Marlon and after we'd done the scene Charlie Chaplin said, For me helping to direct you, it's like I had my hands on the violin and just played the chords. You are wonderful. Listening to Charlie Chaplin saying this to me. I almost fainted."

Brando however, did not enjoy the experience. On his first day he arrived late, and an enraged Chaplin, pacing round the room impatiently, erupted when Brando finally rolled in. "If you're going to be late tomorrow, don't bother coming in again and I will get someone else." Chaplin had originally wanted Cary Grant, but eventually wound up with the less likely Brando, who, it must be added, decided to turn up on time everyday after Chaplin's telling off. "One day I arrived on the set about fifteen minutes late," Brando said. "I was in the wrong and shouldn't have been late, but it happened. In front of the whole cast Chaplin berated me, embarrassing me, telling me that I had no sense of professional ethics and that I was a disgrace to my profession."

He later called Charlie "a monster" and difficult to work with (in his autobiography he wrote that Chaplin was the most sinister man he had ever met), though Loren's account of the film's making in her wonderful autobiography could not be more different.

Tippi Hedren, who has a small role near the end of the film as Ogden's wife, recalled that Chaplin would act out everyone's parts before filming, clearly having the whole film mapped out in his head and being adamant that it would arrive on celluloid as close to that vision as possible. Brando hated this method, while Hedren admired it. "Chaplin's method was to act out all our different roles," she recalled, "which was brilliant to watch. Instead of directing, he'd get out there on set and say: OK, do this, and show us how. He'd become Sophia Loren. He'd become me and Marlon. It was really unusual and I'd never seen it happen before. Can you imagine Marlon Brando handling that? Charlie and Marlon put up with each other, you might say. Marlon was so insulted to see someone acting out his role and that's why he wanted to leave. I thought it was charming and funny but Marlon wanted to quit and Charlie had to convince him to stay on. My take was, you have to look at life with a sense of humour, and the fact that Chaplin went out there and became our characters I thought was delightful. But Marlon wasn't thinking in those terms at all."

But it was also apparently a bright and well humoured set. Loren, ever the professional, was always the first to arrive at the studio, checking the lighting etc. She and Charlie got along like a house on fire. That said, as Charlie had banned all reporters from the set, Loren irritated him somewhat by opening herself up for a number of interviews. Once he began to see her picture plastered over every magazine, he complained to one press agent, "She's getting all the attention!" Still, this minor issue did not ruin their friendship.

Future star of Monty Python, Carol Cleveland, had a small role in A Countess from Hong Kong as a nurse tending to Margaret Rutherford. In 2019 I spoke to Cleveland on the phone about her memories of the set and being directed by Chaplin.

How did you manage to get the part in A Countess from Hong Kong?

Well I got the call from my agent. I think we were filming at Pinewood Studios. I had been doing some work with studios then, and some TV and film bits, and it was my agent who put me up for the part. Whoever the casting agent was probably cast me in a number of things, so I think it was them who just cast me, basically, which was nice.

Did you meet Charlie Chaplin before you got on the set?

No, not before I went on set. And I was on set for a while before I did meet him, I remember. I watched from afar what was going on, a lot of technical stuff really when I arrived. Nothing was being filmed. I remember being very disappointed that Marlon Brando wasn't going to be there that day, because I was a tremendous Marlon Brando fan. But I was happy to see Sophia Loren was there. She was going to be in the next scene after ours. And I just watched her from afar. I did not meet her unfortunately. I hoped I was going to be introduced to her. But I watched her being made up and I just remember looking at her and thinking God you are stunningly beautiful. I thought she was gorgeous. So I did manage to see her but not Marlon. I did not see Charlie until we came to do our scene.

What was it like meeting him? Were you in awe or was it just professional for you?

Oh I was, I was in awe! Marlon, Sophia, all of them. After all it was early days in my career and I was always in awe of every film star I got to work with, because most of them were very pleasant. A couple weren't, but I won't go into it. But when he did arrive, he was lovely, Mr Chaplin. Margaret Rutherford had arrived at the same time for our scene together in the film, so they were setting all that up. There was a bit of time waiting around, as there always is. But then we came to the scene with Margaret, and that was very interesting. I did not have a lot to say in the scene, just a few lines as her nurse. But at the end of the day I was quite glad to have had only a few lines actually, because even though I go to say my lines I was never too sure when and where I was going to be saying them. The scene was rather loosely scripted. I did discover much later on reading about the film, reading one of the reviews, and it said that was actually the way Charlie liked to work. With this particular film anyway, he had a very loose script and he would stand there and go over it with the actors, and then there would be lots of improvising. And when you watch the film I think that becomes quite clear. In this particular scene with Margaret, bless her, there was a lot of fussing and faffing, and mumbling going on. The dear lady. And with Charlie, we ran through the scene a few times and each time it was different, totally different every time. Charlie was quite happy with what we were doing, me and Margaret, so then we went for a break. We had to do it a few times, and as I say it was never quite the same. I never knew quite when she was going to say her lines. I never knew when I was supposed to say mine. It was a very interesting experience. I remember giggling a lot to myself in between takes.

Watching Charlie direct, even though it was loosely structured, was he still in command, having people running around and responding to his orders? Did he seem like that kind of a director?

I think so yes. I mean I was only there for the day, I just saw him doing the scene I was in. Interestingly enough there weren't a lot of people involved. I think there was just one other person involved, the three of us in the scene which was not very long. But as I say he was very calm and relaxed. He came over and basically said let's go through it a couple of times, and then said, fine, let's shoot it. And then it was just a case of faffing the way through the scene.

Was it surreal seeing him come into the room at all? Did it feel like this icon coming in from a different age?

I didn't think of it like that at all really. I was just, as I said, a fan who was delighted to be working with him, having already worked with his son (Sydney). I had had an introduction to the son, so now it was a case of I'm with the dad. And at the time I was more in awe of Marlon and Sophia, to tell you the truth. They were the ones I really wanted to see. But it wasn't until quite a while later that I appreciated how very fortunate I was to be directed by Charlie Chaplin.

Looking back on an experience like this - you are talking about being in a film with Chaplin, Brando and Loren for God's sake - does it ever feel like someone else? As if you ask yourself, was I really there?

I absolutely do look back and ask, did I really experience that? Prior to talking to you today I gave this some serious thought and thought, yes, even this morning, gosh I was lucky. I was so lucky to be doing that. I have been fortunate to work with a lot of big stars. Even though I was in awe, I wasn't star struck if you understand what I mean. Being in awe is different to being star struck standing there gawping. I just felt so lucky, and that's how I feel now, even more so actually.

Oona remained on set everyday and in particular enjoyed observing Margaret Rutherford's scene, laughing hysterically at the rushes featuring the one time Miss Marple no matter how many times she saw them. One day film historian Kevin Brownlow turned up with Gloria Swanson to observe the filming. Swanson was apparently delighted, and said before leaving that seeing Chaplin in action really took her back to the good old days of Hollywood.

When filming ended, everybody went their separate ways. Brando was the first to leave, naturally, and Oona and Charlie took a week's holiday before the edit was to begin. Meanwhile Jerry Epstein began to sort out the rushes.

Though it was clear early on that Chaplin had a flop and a dud on his hands, the finished film is anything but a failure. It is however, almost completely out of touch (not that Charlie wanted to be particularly modern). Released in a time when films were punctuated by hidden meanings and subtext, the film is all text on the surface. A Countess from Hong Kong is like a flashback. The word farce is key of course, because A Countess from Hong Kong is definitely a farce and nothing else. That said, Charlie's main aim, with the statement on power aside, was to apparently make a good romantic film, a genre he insisted never goes out of fashion. But the film is not totally romantic in the truest sense and remains for the most part a broad comedy.

When one watches the film closely, you learn that little has changed from the chaos of Chaplin's earliest shorts, shot fifty years before this glossy production, only dialogue now helps drive along the confusion and whirling mayhem of the film's mix ups and mishaps. There are some genuinely laugh out loud moments throughout, lots of energy which rarely falters, and Chaplin's brief cameo as the head waiter, during a rather choppy moment on the boat where everyone is being sick, is simply wonderful. It's his first and last moment on screen in colour, as well as his final movie moment all together.

Brando, a man known prior to this for his visceral, tough and methodically constructed performances in films like On the Waterfront, The Men and a Streetcar Named Desire, applies himself surprisingly well to the more lightly comedic surroundings, though he does believably portray the more cantankerous side of Ogden better. He is clearly holding back, for Chaplin was famously dominant with his direction of the young method actor, yet he rarely falters in these controlled circumstances. Charlie's son Sydney does very well too, while the actor Patrick Cargill is a stand out in the cast as Ogden's valet, Mr Hudson, who delivers one of the film's funniest scenes when drunk and trying to get cosy in his bed. The real star, for me at least, is the beautiful Sophia Loren, a stunning spectacle in the middle of the slamming doors and scurrying escapes, who is also very funny and effective with whatever Chaplin gives her in the film. Loren had started her decade with an Oscar win in the tough and enthralling Two Women, but here, as she did in some of filmmaker Vittorio De Sica's finest films of the 1960s, displays her knack with comedy. In truth she is the most comfortable and effective person in the film.

The film was not a commercial hit and most of the critics despised it. To them, Chaplin was a man of the past and the film was hopelessly old fashioned, stuck in another age all together. The New York Times were one of the most aggressive with their criticism, writing at the time, "...it is a far cry from the great films that Charlie Chaplin made, even as late as Monsieur Verdoux and Limelight, to the painfully antique bedroom farce he has put together in A Countess From Hong Kong. And if an old fan of Mr. Chaplin's movies could have his charitable way, he would draw the curtain fast on this embarrassment and pretend it never occurred. But that cannot be. We have to face it, not only because it has two such answerable performers as Sophia Loren and Marlon Brando in the leading roles, but also because Mr. Chaplin has indicated his great pride in it, and because it is being presented with splashy éclat. It is so bad that I wondered, at one point, whether Mr. Chaplin, who wrote and directed it, might not be trying to put us on—trying to travesty the kind of hiding-in-the-closet comedies, where people banged on doors and those in the room dived for cover, that were popular as two-reel silent films. But if he was, he failed to surround his story with a sufficiently clever slapstick style, and he certainly failed to communicate his intention to Mr. Brando and Miss Loren."

More recent reviews have criticised the acting, with TV Guide complaining, "Chaplin's story and script employed moth-eaten dialog and static scenes which none of the actors could enliven. Loren spends most of her time teasing Brando and the audience while wearing his silk pyjamas, running in and out of closets and toilets to hide, a peek-a-boo performance that is embarrassing. Her lines are delivered phlegmatically and are almost unintelligible through her thick Italian accent. She is earthy and peasant-like in a role that calls for sophistication and culture. Her unbelievability is matched by Brando, who struts about mouthing diplomatic ambiguities over what Loren's presence will do to his image and career. Chaplin's return to the movies is a sad failure..."

As time has it, A Countess from Hong Kong is viewed not as Charlie's last great heroic cry, but his final cowardly whimper. This is a shame, for I feel it deserves more credit than it unjustly receives.

Yet one cannot view A Countess from Hong Kong without understanding the film landscape in which it was unleashed, especially if one is going to attempt to understand its harsh reception. Let us not forget, 1967 was the year of the arrival of New Hollywood, when Arthur Penn ordered the brutal and bloody on-screen massacre of Warren Beatty and Faye Dunaway's Bonnie and Clyde, when the mavericks snuck through the holes in the fence and temporarily took over the reigns of Hollywood's archaic chariot. In comparison to the new wave of films coming in to theatres that year, such as The Graduate, and the ones to follow, most obviously the likes of Easy Rider and Five Easy Pieces, A Countess from Hong Kong could not have been more stuffy and out of place. In the 1910s or twenties it would have come across as revolutionary and advanced in terms of plot development and camera sets ups, while it would have fit snugly in the Golden Period of the 1930s and 40s. In the mid to late sixties however, it's understandable, despite the vital talents of its two stars, that younger viewers found it unappealing. Thankfully, fifty odd years on, its appreciation has at least grown a little, though it will never enter the ranks of Chaplin's true classics. It is also worth noting that it is one of only two films Chaplin directed and did not star in, the other being 1923's A Woman of Paris, which was also funnily enough a commercial disappointment. Had the films not been credited to Chaplin, then who knows, the critic's expectations might have been lower and the reception kinder.

That's not to say the film is flawless, for it is certainly flawed, despite being enjoyable. The final fifteen to twenty minutes for instance are a bit of a mess, while Loren and Brando's final scene together is unconvincing, especially with the overly sentimental soundtrack, a beautiful piece of music written by Chaplin, intruding over the insincerity of Brando's delivery. Yet it's fun, daft and lovably corny. It's also Chaplin's final film, so whether perfect or not, a masterpiece or a dud, it's of major historical importance.

Charlie was understandably disappointed with the harsh reviews. He told Frances Wyndham during an interview that with his next film he wouldn't open it in London. "I will open in Kalamazoo or somewhere and leave London till later." He went on to criticise London, saying he didn't understand what was going on there. One must remember the London he was speaking of was in the midst of its so called swinging era. "When the swinging thing is over, what will they have left?" he asked. "I don't believe there is such a thing as fashion. Who the hell creates fashion anyway? Anyone can. Cynics - so what? Soon they will come to their senses and start having a good time."

He consoled himself by insisting the reviews for his films had always been mixed, and also revealed that the theme song to A Countess from Hong Kong had ironically become a hit all over the world. He mentioned admiring some recent films, such as Goldfinger, but thought the artier films, in this case Antonioni's Blow Up, were "slow and boring", while also dubbing Doctor Zhivago, among the biggest films of the era no doubt, "banal". (Ironically, his daughter Geraldine had a role in it.)

Speaking to Richard Meryman in 1966, Charlie was willing to discuss his films but not his private life. He talked of his technical tastes, his set habits, but didn't give much away about the magic he had achieved in the past. Bearing in mind he had just made a film in a completely different age and environment to what he was used to, Chaplin explained:"I like the lighting more or less up—I don't like shadows. I don't think it's the most important element in a film. I think if you concentrate on that, you may be neglecting something else. As to the camera, if I have a rule at all, it is the fact that I like to establish orientation—to know where you are. I like to keep the camera way back, then come into a closeup or whatever you want to finish up. You can eliminate time, with discretion, but now they go overboard. I don't mind when they cut away—it's refreshing to me. But I do like to see something smooth. I use the closeup, not in any sense of mechanics, but sort of as an emphasis, as punctuation, like putting in a comma or parentheses. Technique is so much a part of expression through the camera. But I really concentrate more on the performances of the actors."

On the fact that people might find him and his latest film old fashioned, Chaplin said "Well, they all have an idea that I'm terribly conservative and I'm not. We don't twist the camera upside down. Personality, people, the human equation transcend any acrobatics that the camera might do. I don't think there is such a word as being old-fashioned, in the deepest sense, because we don't understand the past, the present; we're conscious of the future. I like the misty mysticism of that. Time is something that is there, and we pretend that everything is modern and new, but it's not. So I'm never bothered about being old-fashioned. Of course, one is so insecure, because you never know what the hell is coming out. It was very fine, very discreet. I rather liked the idea of it. It's like any picture—the only nervous qualms I had was starting. The moment we took the first scene I knew what I wanted."

Meryman also brought up the word genius in his interview, but Chaplin was reluctant to apply it to himself. "I've never known quite what a genius was. I think it's somebody with a talent, who's highly emotional about it, and is able to master a technique. Everybody is gifted in some way. The average man has to differentiate between doing a regular sort of unimaginative job, and the fellow who's a genius doesn't. He does something different, but does this very well. Many a jack-of- all-trades have been mistaken for a genius... but genius is such a pretentious word, and you come to find it doesn't mean anything. You see genius all over the world, in beautiful paintings ... I think they do their job well, and they're artists, and how far the genius goes, some are better artists than others."

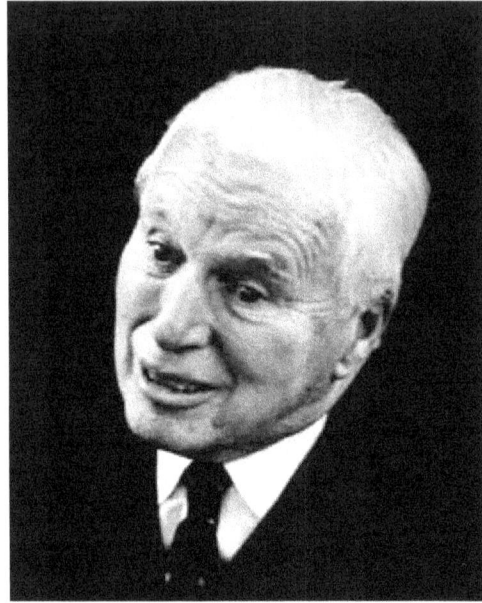

Chaplin in 1965.

Though Chaplin was not in his latest film, save for the cameo, interviewers still brought up his Tramp persona. Speaking of the Tramp's place in modern times, and perhaps addressing why he refused to play him any more, Chaplin said, "I don't think there's any place for that sort of person now. The world has become a little bit more ordered. I don't think it's happier now, by any means. I've noticed the kids with their short clothes and their long hair, and I think some of them want to be tramps. But there's not the same humility now. They don't know what humility is, so it has become something of an antique. It belongs to another era. That's why I couldn't do anything like that now. And of course, sound—that's another reason. When talk came in I couldn't have my character at all. I wouldn't know what kind of voice he would have. So he had to go."

Though accommodating in interviews and playing down the harsh rejection of his film, friends and family say the reaction to the film, as acidic as it often was, hurt him greatly. The film also came out around the same time Michael published his warts and all memoir, which brought embarrassment to Oona and Charlie. Even though the book spoke of Chaplin's more difficult character traits, Michael insisted he adored his parents. He dubbed his father "Complex, gifted, strangely creative... He was and is, to put it mildly, a bit of a handful as a father."

Things began to change around the time he was working on A Countess from Hong Kong. While editing the film, he went out for a walk with Jerry Epstein in the grounds of Pinewood Studios and tripped and fell on a piece of crooked pavement. He was driven off to Slough Hospital where his foot was put in plaster. Chaplin found the whole thing humiliating, and was perhaps aware that at his ripe old age (he was in his mid seventies) an injury like this could seriously slow him down. It was the first chink in his armour so to speak.

Though considered a kind of historical figure, his admirers' love remained undimmed. In 1967 the iconic mime artist Marcel Marceau had a chance meeting with Chaplin, the man who had been his childhood idol and helped inspire him and his act. While waiting for a plane at Orly airport, Marcel's cousin alerted him to the fact that Chaplin, Oona and the children were all sat in the airport cafe, and that Charlie was looking at him. When Marceau built up the courage to approach his hero, Chaplin said "Hello Marcel Marceau. I have seen all your posters in Paris. Children, come and meet Marcel Marceau." Marcel told Chaplin he was a God to him. He then began to mimic the Tramp walk, which prompted Chaplin to do the same. For Marcel it was a magical moment. When Oona urged Charlie to hurry up as they needed to be in Vevey, Marcel saw that Chaplin had tears in his eyes. Marcel saw it as a symbolic meeting. Chaplin had once been unable to move through the streets without being mobbed. "And then nobody recognised him," Marcel recalled. "He had not made films in years and I was not only Marcel Marceau the mime, but a new generation. When I kissed his hand, he thought about time, that he had no more life before him." Marcel saw the meeting as poetic, rather sad, and indeed Chaplin may have seen that his influence was going on into a new generation, that his legacy, as much as he might not have thought so at the time due to the onslaught he had received in America, was very much alive and well.

Towards the end of the decade a real tragedy struck him, the death of his son Charlie Jr. in 1968. He had been born in the mid twenties to Charlie and his second wife Lita Grey, and was only 43 when he died in his mother's house. The death, like that of his brother Sydney, hit Chaplin hard.

Though Chaplin was a happy family man, he was still prone to melancholia, indeed as he had at the height of his fame. Speaking of her father, Geraldine Chaplin recalled his mood might change from day to day, particularly in the festive period, where he was reminded of his sad childhood. "But on Christmas, while my mother was putting amazing presents under the tree for me and my sisters, he sometimes grew melancholic. He said, When I was a child, I got an orange. In good years. His most famous movie character, the Tramp, surely had something to do with that childhood. A completely destitute vagabond, who nonetheless has dignity and manners. For me, that character was always a transfigured version of my father's childhood story: the embodiment of a humanism that couldn't be broken. A man who always stood back up. And who always maintained a sense for beauty and romanticism."

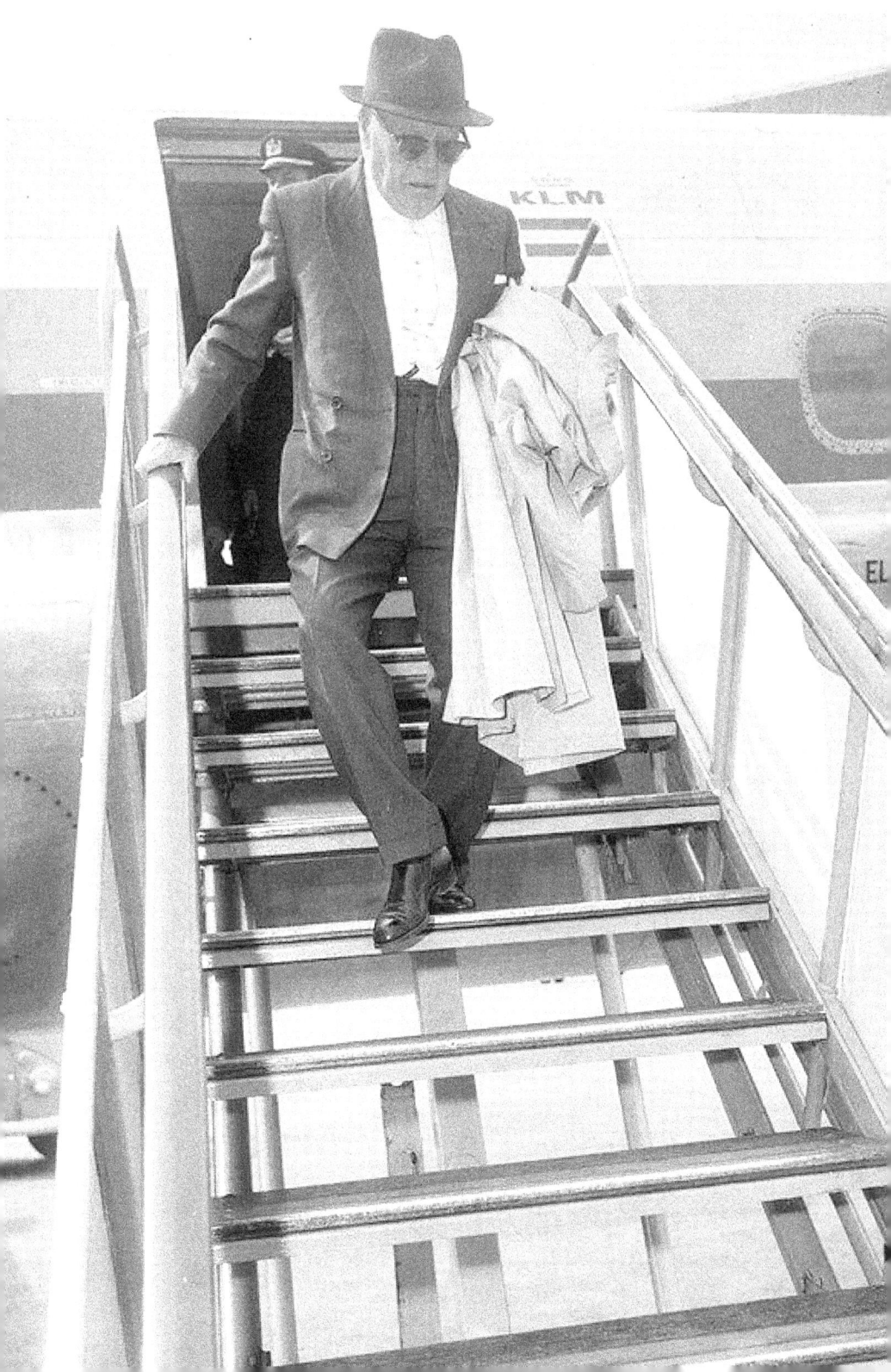

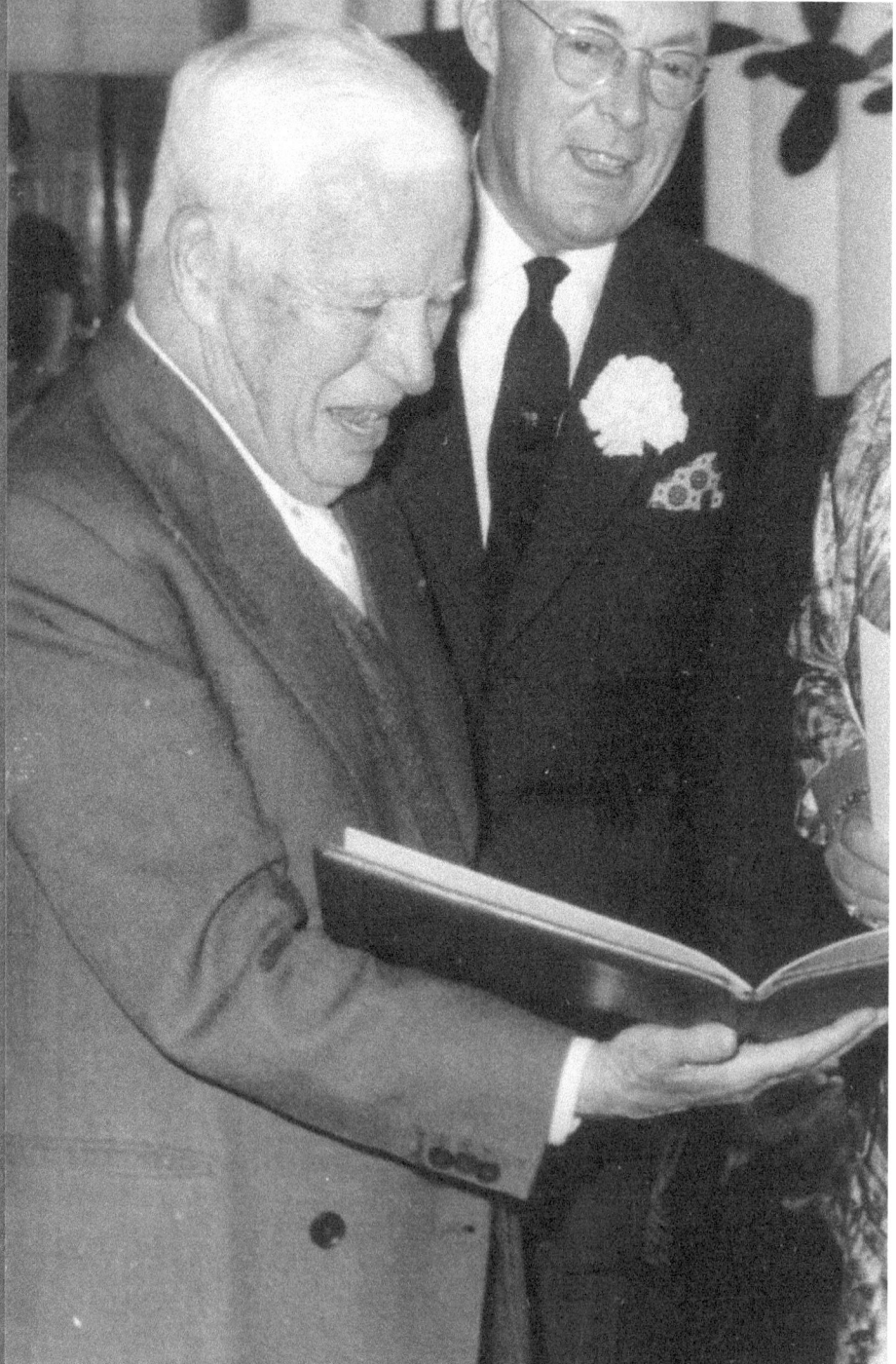

Though slowing down physically, he continued exploring ideas. His next proposed film was The Freak, a project which obsessed him for years. He started serious work on it in 1969, intending it as a vehicle for his daughter Victoria. The story concerned a young girl in South America who suddenly grows wings and is kidnapped. She finds herself in London where her kidnappers plan to make money out of their find. Even when the girl escapes, she is not treated with kindness. Because she is different, she is ostracised and treated like, yes, a freak.

Chaplin was deadly serious about The Freak and put all his energy into it, despite the fact he was 80 during early development. His family and friends knew deep down that Charlie just didn't have the energy to take on another film, but didn't have the heart to tell him. Even by 1974, when he published the wonderful My Life in Pictures book, the final image of him working in his study has a caption regarding The Freak, still insisting that he planned to make it one day. He had the wings made, took pictures of Victoria in costume and even held auditions in London for supporting roles. Charlie shot footage of Victoria in their garden wearing the wings, and Michael later recalled that his father got out of his wheelchair to tell her where she was going wrong. "He became a film director again," Michael added.

But it was not to be. Victoria suddenly met a man and got married, and she wasn't sure the acting life was for her. Alas, the film was never made, which is frustrating, for documents show that it would have been another masterpiece, perhaps his finest film since The Great Dictator or even earlier.

"It seemed to me to be a very beautiful fairytale. Something that maybe only a man of his age can imagine, can dream. A very charming dream," Michael Chaplin told AFP in 2015. Author Pierre Smolik, who penned a book on the doomed project, said of the screenplay: "When reading it, one can glimpse what this 'Freak' would have been: a subtle mixture of the tale, the fable, the dream, the amusing, tender or satirical comedy, black humour, the tragedy, the nightmare, suspense, poetry."

Insistent he was still going to make it, even as his frailty overtook him, even Chaplin had to admit the dream was over as his health worsened and the script disappeared into time. Still, the footage of Victoria in the wings, fluttering around the grounds of the Manoir de Ban, sends a chill up the spine and suggests what the film might have been had he taken it on ten or so years earlier.

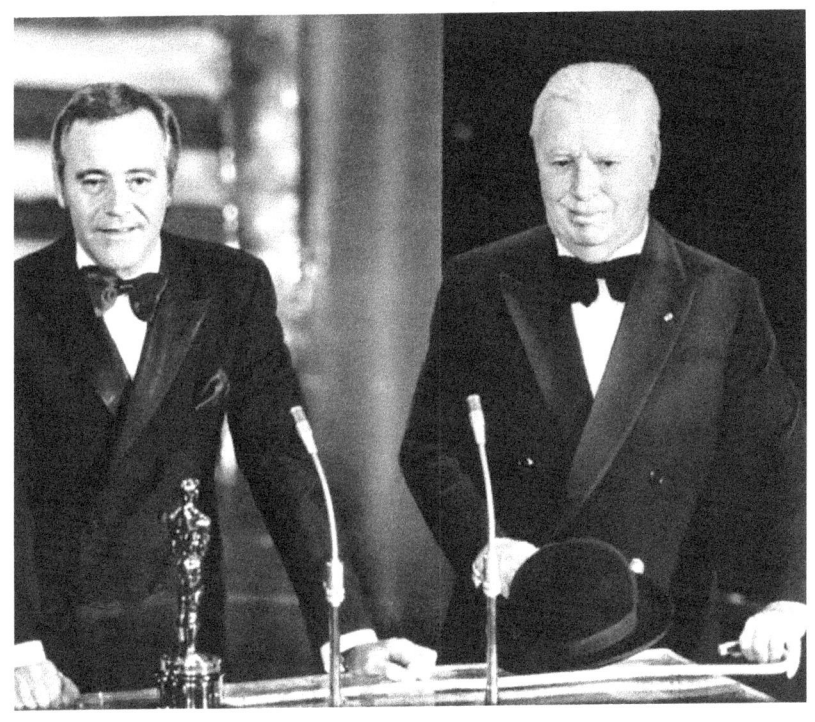

The Final Years

Things were really slowing down as the sixties morphed into the seventies, and Chaplin, now aged 80, was beginning to fade away. His well known vitality was disappearing, but he had not yet given up. Though he was no longer seriously attempting to explore new film ideas, he was still very much invested in his old masterpieces. At the turn of the decade he was exploring new deals for the distribution rights to his films, with both Jerry Epstein and his son Sydney putting themselves forward as hopefuls to take over such affairs. Though old, Charlie was still formidable and prone to standing up for himself. One time Sydney turned up at the Manoir de Ban with the producer Sandy

Lieberson, with a view of talking to Charlie, who knew nothing of the meeting, about possible sales abroad. Chaplin was offended by Sydney's forthrightness and the whole household erupted into an argument - and rightly so. Clearly, Sydney had crossed a line. Instead, Rachel Ford set up a deal with Moses Rothman, who started a new company to distribute Chaplin's movies in the USA, where half of all proceeds would go to Chaplin's Roy Export Company. Once again, Ford stepped up to the plate. As part of the deal, Chaplin agreed to make the odd promotional appearance to support re-releases of his films, this also ensuring he had a continued interest in his past work and went on composing new scores for them. In 1971 he cut new scores for both The Kid and The Idle Class, and the music was as effective as anything he'd created before.

David Robinson, noted film critic and future Chaplin biographer, had managed to get himself into various Chaplin press conferences through the fifties and sixties. He recalled being at the event Charlie hosted announcing his plans to make A Countess from Hong Kong, but admitted he didn't build up the courage to ask the great man a question. In the seventies however, after writing an article about the re-release of Limelight, and shedding some light (no pun intended) on the music hall backdrop against which the film was set, Robinson received a pleasant surprise. In 2019 he told me, "In the New Year I got a card in the post signed Charlie and Oona Chaplin. I thought it was a joke. People know I like Charlie Chaplin, so someone's having a gag with me. On the bottom it was signed 'We loved your review of Limelight, Charlie and Oona Chaplin.' And then I thought, OK, maybe it's real! So I made so bold as to call the Chaplin secretary to say thank you very much and how touched I was. And then I forgot about that. Kept the card of course, still got the card!"

1971 was also the year the Cannes Film Festival decided to honour the great man. The French had always loved Chaplin, indeed had most of Europe, so such plaudits were expected. More unexpected was the 1972 Oscars tribute to Chaplin, organised by long time admirer Peter Bogdanovich. Chaplin did not see himself ever going back to America again, but now he was older a lot of the grudges had faded, and he was genuinely moved to be invited by the Academy.

Bogdanovich recalled the events which led to Charlie coming from Switzerland for the tribute evening: "Burt Schneider, who produced The Last Picture Show, was bringing Charlie Chaplin's pictures out again, for the first time in ages. So the Academy was going to help promote those re-releases by giving Chaplin a special Oscar. Burt called me and asked if I would do the montage of Chaplin clips to introduce Charlie's arrival back to this country after 20 years in exile. So I said Sure. I knew Chaplin's pictures pretty well, so it didn't take long. I went through the ones I wanted as an editor, and put it together pretty quickly."

As the montage was 13 minutes long, the Academy said it was too lengthy to be shown. Burt told them Chaplin would not come unless they screened the reel, so finally they agreed.

Bogdanovich recalled his other memories of Chaplin: "I had never met Chaplin before he came to Hollywood for the Oscars tribute, but we were in communication beforehand. In fact, he gave us all the old films I used for the clip reel. They came directly from Charlie. I actually sent him the montage to see if he liked it before I sent it to the Academy, and he came back and said he wanted a clip from The Great Dictator in it, because there wasn't one — it's not one of my favorite films — but he wanted a shot of the dictator bouncing the world as a balloon. So we put that in. And that was his only comment."

When Chapline received a two week visa for his visit to the States, his family were outraged, offended even. Charlie though, smiled, and mischievously added, "They're still scared of me." Charlie and Oona flew first to New York. Charlie had been nervous about coming to America but was overwhelmed by his reception. When they screened The Idle Class and The Kid at an event four days before the Oscars night, Chaplin was moved, stating from the stage: "First, thank you for your wonderful applause. It is so very gratifying to know that I have so many friends," he said. "It's easy for you but difficult for me to speak tonight, as I feel very emotional. I'm glad to be among so many friends. Thank you."

The next day he and Oona went through Central Park and had dinner at the 21 cafe. Old friends visited his hotel suite and the Mayor of New York gave him the Handell medallion, the highest honour of the city. He spent the rest of the week in the big apple before flying to Hollywood with Oona, accompanied by Candice Bergen who was writing a piece on Chaplin for Life Magazine. She reported Charlie's excitement when the plane passed the grand canyon, and like a child he rushed to the other side of the plane to peer down at it. He began to feel more nervous as they got closer to LA. "Oh well," he was heard to say, "I did meet Oona there after all."

When he arrived he learned that the new owners of his film studio had decorated the place with flags and banners with Chaplin's face on them. Apparently, overcome with emotion, Charlie could not face the greeting he would receive there, or the old studio itself where he had crafted so many glorious masterpieces. Later on, when it was closed, he went over and peered solemnly through the gates at his old work place. At the weekend he lunched with old friends, some of whom he did not appear to recognise. Over awed by all the people around him, Charlie was having a few seconds chat here and a few seconds small talk there. Tim Durant, an old friend who was at the dinner, was upset when he assumed Charlie did not recognise him. However, near the end of the event Charlie leaned over and quietly said "Tim, you and I were friends once" Tim was terribly moved by the moment.

Charlie built himself up for Oscar night. Once again, Bogdanovich had vivid memories of the evening: "Then the Academy told me that Charlie couldn't walk down the stairs, so I just said why don't we have the screen that shows the montage fly up at the end and he's just standing there? The place will go nuts. So that's what they did. Thirteen and half minutes of film ending with a four-minute sequence from The Kid which would make a stone cry. Believe me, I was there, the whole place was crying! It was this heartbreaking scene between Charlie and young Jackie Coogan. And then the final shot was the last image of The Circus, when Charlie just walks away. The place went nuts, the people just started cheering, the screen went up, Charlie was there, everybody stood up, and the place went berserk. It was the longest standing ovation I've ever seen."

When Chaplin stepped out on to the stage after a wonderful introduction, Chaplin kept it short and sweet. "Words seem so futile, so feeble," he said, quietly, and concluding with, "You are wonderful, sweet people. Thank you." Chaplin was handed a bowler hat and cane, and attempted to mimic his old Tramp character, but the years were clearly getting the better of him and he dropped the hat. Still, the moment was captured on film and remains one of the most touching in award ceremony history.

The Los Angeles Times published a nice article on the event: "After a 20-year exile in Europe, Charlie Chaplin returned to Hollywood to receive an honorary Oscar on April 10, 1972, for such comedies as The Kid, The Gold Rush, City Lights, Modern Times and The Great Dictator. Chaplin, then 82, received probably the longest standing ovation in the history of the Oscar telecast as he walked slowly to the podium to pick up his Academy Award for his incalculable effect in making motion pictures the art form of the century. Chaplin was quite literally speechless as he looked at the throng of stars whose cheers kept getting louder. He finally uttered thank you so much, referring to the audience as sweet people. And there wasn't a dry eye in the house when Jack Lemmon gave him his famous Little Tramp hat and cane."

After his moving but short speech, Bogdanovich approached Chaplin at the Governer's Ball. Introducing himself as the man he had been in touch with for the past few weeks and had put together the montage, Chaplin's only comment was "Jackie Coogan.. He was a little boy and now he's a fat old man." Embarrassed, Peter did not know what to say. Finally Oona broke the silence and said how good the tribute was. "Yes," Charlie mumbled, "yes, very good, very good."

Chaplin later wrote in his book My Life in Pictures, that it was a touching event, adding with subtlety, "but there was an irony about it somehow..."

The same year he was receiving other honours, such as the Golden Lion at the Venice Film Festival. During the event St Mark's Square was turned into a Chaplin party, and they screened City Lights in the open air. Chaplin was all set up to stand on the balcony and wave to the crowd just before the film started, but he was slightly delayed in doing so, having watched a bit of his film, which he evidently enjoyed.

When he returned to Switzerland he started work on the book My Life in Pictures, to be released in 1974. Compiling his favourite pictures, both from his life and his movies, he wrote new captions to go under each. The book is wonderful and a perfect companion to the autobiography. The images are fabulous of course but Chaplin's texts are like little nuggets of gold. Later in the year he visited London for the launch of the book and happily gave interviews. He insisted to reporters that he would never be able to properly retire because ideas refused to stop entering his head. But he was 85 at the time and sadly no more films were to come to fruition.

Then Chaplin received the news that he would be granted a knighthood. The poor little boy from London had finally made it. Journeying from Switzerland, obviously a big task at the time, and reaching London with his family, Chaplin waited in Buckingham Palace as the orchestra played the theme from A Countess from Hong Kong, before going into a rendition of Chaplin's classic song Smile (originally from his film, Modern Times) as he went for his knighthood from the Queen. Unable to walk all the way, he was wheeled towards her royal highness, who apparently told Chaplin that his films had meant a great deal to her and had helped her through the years. Outside he posed for pictures and answered reporters' questions, though his replies were vague in comparison to his earlier press statements.

When Charlie received his knighthood, film critic David Robinson was surprised to get a call from Chaplin's secretary Miss Ford: "This dragon lady who was their secretary and sort of bodyguard... They were scared of her too, she was such a dragon lady! She was wonderful. So she called me and said 'We are having a little party at the Savoy to celebrate and we wondered if you'd like to come. It's only a little get together, nothing special and mostly family, but we wondered if you'd like to come.' So I said I would very much like to come, of course, and I was there. It was a family affair, very much so. And... there he was! But by this time he was certainly declining in health and one could see the mind was going OK, even if he found it hard to communicate. He was just sitting there quietly. If you spoke to him he would not respond or even seem to hear what you said. The family knew this, so they didn't bother him and left him alone. He was sat on a sofa and I sat beside him. For most of the party we were sat together. It was very interesting because the mind was working, but when one asked him something the answer then came none. But his eyes never left this small boy, and I never discovered whose child he was. I suppose he must have been one of the grandchildren. He was a little boy with very bright red, very curly hair. And Charlie was fascinated by him. The little boy came over and stood in front of him, and Charlie reached out with his fingers and fingered the hair. Then the little boy ran away again and Charlie's eyes followed him. And then, having been so uncommunicative, he took my arm and said 'You see, they always gravitate towards the mother.' And this was rather a startling sentence, having finding him so uncommunicative. Then there was a call from 10 Downing Street, and the prime minister asked if he might be able to come down and offer his congratulations. It was Harold Wilson, he'd actually organised the whole thing. He admired Chaplin very much. And Harold Wilson came into the room and suddenly the old Charlie was renewed. He stood up, went forward and shook the hand with a bright smile. It was an amazing transformation. And then Wilson turned to someone else and Charlie was left there and absolutely subsided again and had to be taken back to his chair. It was very sad to see his decline, but Oona was defying it and would not let anyone acknowledge that he was not what he once was. But it was very strange because that person that he had been was somewhere inside there."

Charlie then went to Anvil Studios in London to supervise the recording of the new music he had written and composed for A Woman of Paris. Given that the film had been received such a mute reception upon release, and that he had barely spoken of it in the following decades, it was quite remarkable that Chaplin was revisiting what many saw as a failed project. Once again, David Robinson was invited to come along, having received a phone call from Miss Ford.

"He needed a lot of help from the arranger," Robinson told me, "and they used a lot of his old music. I mean, it is certainly not one of his best scores and is not as successful, however it is his! And we went there and sat in a little observational room outside from where the orchestra was playing. Obviously he was not contributing much but he was watching with some interest. Oona and MIss Ford were there, then they went off and left us alone, just the two of us. Again he was not communicative, but again could just spark up. I tried to talk to little response, and then I said, Did it take long to write the music for this? And suddenly the old Chaplin was back. He said, Not long, inspiration mostly! A nice phrase. Then a daughter came in, one of the younger ones. I'm not sure which one now, but he suddenly said, May I present to you, my daughter? Very sprightly. And then we sat some more and the orchestra broke and we were looking through the window at them. Then two of the musicians pretended to fight. This he found very disturbing and very frightening. He said I want to go home! I want to go home! So I went and got Oona and Miss Ford and they took him home. He was frightened."

I asked David if, even though Chaplin was but a shell at this point, he was still aware of being sat next to Charlie Chaplin, the legend himself, and whether he had an aura. "Of course he had an aura," laughed David. "Even if I invented it he had an aura. It was one of the greatest moments of my life."

In 1975 the documentary The Gentleman Tramp saw release. Featuring up to date footage of the elderly Chaplin at home in Vevey, holding hands and walking the grounds with Oona, it's a tremendously moving and heartfelt piece, essential viewing for anyone looking for a glimpse into Chaplin's later home life - and another chance to view classic scenes from his old masterpieces. The same year, Peter Bogdanovich had visited Vevey to interview Chaplin in his home about his life. Footage of this is rather upsetting to watch. When Peter brings up Mack Sennett (the man who signed him to Keystone Pictures in 1914, sixty years earlier no less) and Fred Karno (the man who gave him his stage break), Chaplin appeared to have no memory of them at all. He did, however, recall minute details of his tragic childhood. Even senility had not blown away the dust of those memories.

Chaplin's final months were spent relaxing with family at home in Vevey. Eugene says they often put on his old films, and whenever the children laughed at particularly funny moments, Charlie would sit upright in his chair and smile too. Sylvester Stallone, who had recently scored big with Rocky, wanted to meet Charlie and through Jerry Epstein arranged for a print of the film to be sent out to the Manoir de Ban. Though no meet up was ever set in place, Charlie and the family did screen Rocky. Charlie enjoyed it, muttering every now and then, "Excellent... excellent." Rocky and the Tramp didn't cross paths, but they admired each other's work for sure. He also reportedly viewed a print of what was then Stanley Kubrick's latest feature, Barry Lyndon, which he found beautiful. The image of an elderly Chaplin, sat watching such a film, is certainly a very moving and haunting one.

Eugene also said that though he had not permitted them to watch TV when they were very small, he now had a more relaxed attitude towards it. Gout limited his physical life, so he happily sat with the family watching the French news and mimicking the actors in films. Geraldine recalled he would sit before the fire, in both summer and winter, for hours on end. When Oona tried to get him outdoors he would often refuse and say "it's my only luxury." Eugene says a lot of TV was watched in the final weeks and his last appearance on film was at the Harvest Wine Festival, where a frail Charlie in large black rimmed spectacles smiles as the children frolic. Other times he sat for hours with Oona, often not saying a word but always holding hands. The driver would take them to the river, where the happy couple would relax until sundown. Then they would be taken back to the Manoir de Ban. It seems to have been a peaceful, even idyllic final chapter in the great man's wonderful life.

In the middle of October 1977 he made his last trip out of the house when he and the family and some local friends went to see the Circus Knie. After this he went speedily down hill, needing constant care and attention. Still, he seemed happy, most of all because Oona and the children were always close by.

On Christmas Eve 1977, Oona invited all the children that had moved away for a celebration back at the Manoir de Ban. Michael recalls coming through the door to a mountain of gifts and a joyous atmosphere. Charlie, though not well, was sat in the corner enjoying himself. By evening however he felt unwell and asked to be taken upstairs. He also requested the door be left open so he could hear the joy of the children as they opened their gifts. The next morning, in what Michael Chaplin called perfect timing, Charlie Chaplin passed away peacefully. The Little Tramp had waddled off for the final time, but he would never, ever be forgotten.

It's forty three years since Charlie Chaplin died, but his legacy remains undimmed. Though his reputation took a down turn in the 80s when cynical critics began over emphasising his sugary qualities, and enhanced the films of Buster Keaton as higher art than Chaplin's, now Charlie's status seems immovable. His later years, though nowhere near as iconic as his classic era (how could they be?), were also a wonderful time, producing key pictures like Limelight, a host of fine film soundtracks, many illuminating interviews, two autobiographical books, much press and home footage reflecting his activities, plenty of happy, uplifting tales and a feeling that all was right in Chaplin's world, finally, after decades of ups and downs. Chaplin did once emphasise the fact he was an entrance and exit man (who had a better on screen entrance than him, not to mention the classic Tramp waddle off at the end of Modern Times), and given his "king in exile" state in the latter days, his exit was a fine one too. He could not have been further from the destitute, gritty streets of late 19th century London, living effectively a life of luxury in Switzerland, but his past remained with him always. Even at his happiest he carried an air of melancholia, a visible sign of the strain his earliest years had taken on him. And it is this which makes Charlie, and indeed the best of us, so human, fragile, real and relatable. Chaplin, old man or young, is a figure we can all learn from.

When Geraldine Chaplin was asked recently what she would say to her father now, if he could come back, she urged him to stay where he was, for the world was a changed, scary, often horrible place. She had a point of course, for what place is there now, on this drastically altered earth, for such a gentle soul as he? But though she wished him to remain in the afterlife, Geraldine urged that he let us keep the Tramp. After all, we need him more than ever.

References and Acknowledgements

I would like to thank David Robinson and Carol Cleveland for sharing their memories of Chaplin.

The following books were useful;
His Life and Art, by David Robinson
Chaplin, by Peter Ackroyd
My Life in Pictures, by Charles Chaplin
My Autobiography, by Charles Chaplin
Charlie Chaplin: The Complete Film Guide, by Chris Wade

The following documentaries;
Chaplin: His Life and Work
Stealing Chaplin
The Unknown Chaplin
Charlie Chaplin: The Making of a Genius
Chaplin biography documentary
Chaplin: The Forgotten Years
Chaplin in Ireland
The Gentleman Tramp
A Legend of the Century

The following magazines and websites;
Charlie Chaplin archives
New York Times
New York Review
Variety
Hollywood Reporter
Life
Time

ABOUT CHRIS WADE

Chris Wade is a UK based writer, filmmaker and musician. As well as running the acclaimed music project Dodson and Fogg, he has written books on The Kinks, Malcolm McDowell, Captain Beefheart, Marcello Mastroianni, Robert De Niro and many others. He has also released audiobooks of his comedic fiction, such as Cutey and the Sofaguard, narrated by Rik Mayall. His other projects include Hound Dawg Magazine, for which he has interviewed such people as Sharon Stone, Donovan and Jethro Tull's Ian Anderson. His art films include The Apple Picker (winning Best Film at the Sydney World Film Festival, and featuring Toyah Willcox and Nigel Planer), and he's made documentaries on George Melly, Lindsay Anderson, Charlie Chaplin and Orson Welles.

More info at his website: wisdomtwinsbooks.weebly.com

www.ingramcontent.com/pod-product-compliance
Lightning Source LLC
Chambersburg PA
CBHW070050210526

45170CB00012B/655

* 9 7 8 0 2 4 4 8 7 4 7 2 8 *